DEACON'S CROSSBOW

By David G. Brown

Brave Down Books

Brave Down Books
7302 Huntsmen Circle 16-D
Anchorage AK 99518

Second Edition
Printed in the United States

Library of Congress Control Number: 2012956071
ISBN 978-0-9854429-1-0

http://promotiondesigns.net/deaconscrossbow

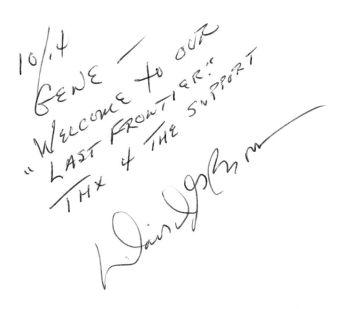

Deacon's Crossbow is dedicated to
my hero, Agnes Smith,
and her husband, Ed,
Don's aunt and uncle.

Table of Contents

Chapter

THINKING AND WRITING OUT LOUD

It's been eighteen years since the Donald Graham and Michael Blodgett confrontation. Part of each day, guaranteed, I wallow in a warped world of anguish, knowing Donald remains in prison due to his sentencing for first degree murder / life without parole. I've become possessed and obsessed, forever curious and filled with angst, over his unfortunate fate. Funny, but I also ponder why I've expended so much energy on his behalf. I suspect not many people would. Most folks, over time, would give up the crusade and go on with their lives. Don is my friend. And it's been that way from the very first day I met him. I was drawn to his sense of humor, convictions and honesty. His straight-ahead approach to everything he espoused earned my respect. Don is my friend.

Other than soldiers who have fought in war, I've never ever been close to someone who's killed another human being. The mere thought takes me to an eerie and obtuse place. You'd think, being an Alaskan, I'd have a better handle on termination; surrounded by so many hunters of moose and bear, all locked and loaded and ready to fire away. Can't relate. Cannot relate with soldiers, street gangsters, poachers, hitmen, even those who kill cows in the slaughterhouses. What I'm getting at, I'd feel remorse, sadness, and guilt looking into the cow's eyes.

Now, I'll tell you a devastating story about life and death!

Chapter One

What Happened?

October 2006

Alien thoughts and images coursed my mind with every roll of the wheels as I traveled along Interstate 95. Earlier, while driving along Benefit Street in Providence, I glanced off to the west and in the distance saw the Rhode Island state capitol, a replica of our nation's capitol building in Washington. Atop the white marble dome stands a solitary figure like a Minuteman from the Revolutionary War. He's called "The Independent Man," a state symbol from the early days of Rhode Island's history. Today, I see him as a stark irony because, in short order, I'll be with the most independent man I've ever known.

I pulled into a service station at Fort Devens and purchased a pack of Marlboro Reds along with a tin of spearmint Altoids. Cost six bucks for that box of cancer sticks. Not proud of myself; haven't smoked in over two years.

Back on the road, I light up, draw, hold the smoke momentarily, and inhale. The first drag tastes just awful and makes me woozy. The second tastes better.

It's mid-October, a time of year when New England autumn foliage reigns supreme. It feels good. It's a nice time to be above the grass. I'm driving north with a destination of Shirley, Massachusetts. Along Interstate 95 and Route 2, I watch the brilliant pastels of the trees pass in front of a clear blue sky. Wild geese fly overhead in synchronized formation, filling me with a sense of freedom, until I arrive on the property of the Souza-Baranowski Correctional Center (SBCC).

I'm here to visit one of the SBCC's most noted residents, Donald S. Graham, a man I've known for more than twenty years and who will be my friend for the duration. He is one of those "throw the mold away" characters who always delivers the goods with no pretenses, which means he's a man of honesty — to a fault — in contrast to this world flooded with fools and careless liars.

Entering the crowded parking lot, I spot an unmarked, occupied, surveillance car on the side of the road. The driver is scanning the area with eagle eyes. In the near corner of the parking lot there's another, more official looking truck with Massachusetts decals. I talk to the driver, who's a courteous and serious female guard in uniform. She's waiting for an ambulance to arrive. Apparently something went wrong inside the walls.

I park. I defy anyone *not* to be nervous while going into a prison, whether you live inside or outside the walls. Stranger still, I'm feeling guilty for just being there, as though they're waiting for me. The SBCC is a maximum security, concrete prison that opened its doors in 1998. It's named after James Souza and Alfred Baranowski, two law enforcers who were killed in 1972 at the MCI Norfolk (Massachusetts) prison during an escape attempt by a convicted murderer. Trust me, this is no Pollyanna place, no country club. Everyone has their game face on. Everything is serious business. This *is* where the elephants go to die.

I'm nervous and anxious. I light up another Red and take two deep pulls, all the while focusing on four names. Donald and Sandra Graham, Michael David Blodgett, and Robert Astin. The four participants. Don and his wife Sandra driving in their car, Blodgett driving Astin in the other. I know so much about this foursome, it's like they're my relatives. Then again, there's so much I don't know. Today that will change. By the time I leave the SBCC, Don will have shared copious, stark details of the entire incident.

One last drag. I squash out the cigarette, wipe a few stray ashes off my shirt, and pop an Altoid. Stepping out of the car, I pause and look out at this imposing fortress. What unexpected protocol awaits? What's expected of me? What do I say to Don? How will Don look?

While walking to the visitor's building, I gain an exterior panavision of the entire complex. The high, rectangular stone wall is completely topped with razor-edged barbed wire. And there's another layer of barbed wire atop the first, only this layer is wheel-shaped. Imposing and intimidating sentry boxes stand at each corner. Movies like *Birdman of Alcatraz* and *Cool Hand Luke* weave through my mind.

The nervousness and guilt continue while I complete my visitor's application in the waiting room. The guard instructs me to take a seat. The large room is busy with about fifty other anxious visitors. Mostly all women; I'm surrounded by mothers, young wives, and children. Each, I surmise, with a dismal tale of woe. I'm moved by their openness and melancholia, veiled humor and pathos. A priest stands near the window with clipboard in hand, filling out forms. I feel way out of place and read the prison rules and regulations.

There's time to ponder; time to get composed. Again, I have visions of Donald and Sandra, Blodgett and Astin. Their unlikely affair. After all the trading of mail, the moment is about to arrive when I'll actually be face to face with my friend. It's been thirteen long years since we last met.

I follow the second hand around the black and white clock on the black and white painted wall. Same clock as grade school. A half hour later my name is called and I snap to attention. I'm directed to a door that opens automatically into the shakedown room where a female guard is in charge. I think she'd be an odds-on favorite against Mike Tyson. She has me remove my belt and shoes. The rules and regs have prepared me for shakedown, and before entering, I placed my wallet and keys in a safety deposit box in the waiting room. Costs a quarter. Visitors are not allowed to have anything in their possession; no jewelry, no wallet, can't even wear a sweater. The guard checks the bottom of my feet. She has me run my hands inside my pants at the belt line, open my mouth wide, and turn my pockets inside out. When she sees a handkerchief, she tells me to return to the waiting room. What?

Back in the waiting room, I place the handkerchief in my safety deposit box. Costs another quarter. Another half hour drags by. Donald and Sandra Graham, Blodgett and Astin —.

After passing the second shakedown, I walk down a long, shiny-floored corridor with barred windows to my right. I can see out to the vacant gravel yard and the barbwired wall. Soon I'm stationed in front of another secured door. It automatically opens. A guard sitting behind a desk looks me over, checks out the room, and instructs me to sit in the Blue Section. "Don't cross your legs. Don't put your arm around the back of the prisoner's chair. Don't touch the prisoner."

I wait in a simple, uncomfortable, plastic, blue chair with no arm rests and bolted to the floor. There are five rows in each section with ten chairs per row. Room capacity is about 100 seats, not including the guard desk set on an elevated platform. A restroom is strategically located along the front wall; visitors are allowed access only if accompanied by a guard. The ceiling is high with sun streaming through the glass roof. Guards meander about, ordering guests to uncross their legs and look straight ahead. It's not a hard and fast rule, because I see people holding hands. What are the officials to do, charge them with a felony?

Sitting in front of me is a prisoner with his visiting wife and son. The boy is about five years old, packed with energy, reminding me of Sammy Davis Jr. when he was a kid performing on stage. The convict, who looks to be in his late twenties, is wearing a neatly pressed orange jumpsuit, just like I've seen in so many movies. On his back are the stenciled letters, D O C. All the inmates wear those letters. This guy's in shape; must spend considerable time in the weight room. He's bald and clean-shaven, except for a trimmed goatee. Put him into a Brooks Brothers suit and he passes for a mortgage broker. I can tell the little boy adores his father by the way they hug, by the way the kid stays close. The wife is tall and slim with eyeglasses, dressed in Islamic garb, a robe to her feet. She's all smiles, very talkative and making her husband laugh. I imagine, outside these walls, she's sad and short on humor. Through-out the room couples are paired off and deep in conversation. Most are animated, urgency dictating their behavior.

There's Don. His entrance appears theatrical, like an off-Broadway play. He enters stage right and quick-paced, walking from a door near the guard station. He spots me sitting in the Blue Section, smiles, and advances.

I'll be damned if he doesn't look good, better than thirteen years ago. Hair neatly combed back, still wearing those thick eyeglasses. He's put on weight, the face is fuller, no longer gaunt. My first thought is one of callous humor that prison life is treating him too good.

For a moment Donald just stands there as though posing for a passport photo, dressed in those god-awful orange prison clothes, the tee shirt yellowed and sneakers worn. I could hardly read the faded D O C on his back.

He walks over to me. We experience a moment of awkward silence. I stand. We hug, breaking the no-touching rule. We sit.

"You have more hair than I do."

"This place keeps me young, Dave."

"Not for nuthin' my friend, you've gone from a welterweight to a light heavyweight."

"Yes I have, but I could never go ten rounds." We laugh. "That's what three squares a day will do for you."

"By the way, I baked you a pineapple upside-down cake, brought a box of cannoles, and a Swiss knife. The bastards wouldn't let me take any of it through shakedown."

"Believe me, they keep a close eye on incoming goodies."

The conversation paused. We looked at each other in disbelief, as if to say, "What the hell are we doing in this place?"

"Are you OK, Don?"

"I am." His look was insincerely sober. "Making the best of a shit situation."

We continue to small talk, reminiscing the old days, people and places. Don is still very talkative and lucid. Thank God.

"So, my friend, what the hell happened?" I held my breath.

"That's a loaded question."

"I want to hear it all."

He lowered his head. "Too much has happened, David. I relive the night of Sunday, February 20, 1994 on a daily basis. If I could just tweak a few frames. Then the trial. What my family has gone through. Sandra. And *this* fucking place." He raised his eyebrows. "I've gone through hell and back."

"I'm sorry."

"I know you are and I'm grateful for that." He frowned and opened his folded hands. "So, where do you want me to begin?"

"Let's go with February 20th."

"Every detail?"

"That would be good."

"I can do that." He looked off for just a moment, then back to me. "You know that Sandra and I had driven up to Canton for round dance lessons at the Trinity Episcopal Church?"

"Yes, I do."

He nodded. "OK. When we got out to the parking lot after class that Sunday evening, I remember Sandy saying, 'This is not good.' And I asked, 'What's the matter?'

"She was warm from the exercise and cold from the winter air. I told her we'd be home soon. 'A nice shower and warm cup of tea will fix you right up.' I then asked if she had a headache. Always worried about that. Since her early twenties Sandra suffered from uveitis, a form of rheumatoid arthritis affecting the eyes.

"But I knew not even a headache could rain on her parade. Not that day.

Sandy was in good spirits because we clicked during our advanced class. While other couples struggled and bickered, we moved across the parquet dance floor like Fred and Ginger. It was one of our best dance days. To celebrate, we drove across the street and had dinner at Howard Johnson's."

"HoJo's has become a name of antiquity." We both smiled.

"An hour later we were on the road. Sandy fell right off to sleep. Most nights she'd be bothered by oncoming headlights, a part of the uveitis malaise. She described the glare as 'looking into a snowstorm.'"

"Poor Sandra. I never knew."

"Oh yes, she dealt with it as best she could." He nodded. "She did."

Donald's countenance took on a melancholy look. I sensed he was thinking of Sandra. There was a squinting pain in his eyes, less bravado in his voice. He paused, then looked up pensively. "I guess we can call that the prologue."

"Fair enough."

"It takes only a few minutes to get from Howard Johnson's to Interstate 95. I turned on the radio, WBZ. I liked that station. Remember the Larry Glick show?"

"Sure do."

He continued. "I set the cruise control at 55 miles per hour and settled into the inside lane. I was in no hurry. With moderate traffic I'm back to Woonsocket in forty-five minutes.

"It's funny, but I remember as soon as we hit I-95 I became very thoughtful. Actually, my mind was racing, much more than usual. I turned the radio off. I thought about the kids, our church, my friend Paul Dempster. I focused on the day's dancing session. I saw myself holding Sandra's hand, how gracefully she curtsied under my arm during a bridge in the music. I remember looking over at her in the car, sitting there with her head tilted back, a gentle, peaceful smile outlining her face. 'That's my girl,' I said to myself."

"You remember all of this?"

"Vividly."

"Were those thoughts important in the whole scheme of things?"

"I don't know. Maybe, maybe not. But you asked me to tell you everything."

"Yes. Good. Keep going."

"I thought about my Toyota. Earlier in the day John Skowron joked about the squeaky door. I wish that was the only problem. The thing was fast becoming a dilapidated piece of shit. On the way up, it conked out twice.

"I turned the radio back on. While setting the volume soft, I happened to look off to my left and noticed a vehicle in the passing lane. Got my attention because it was going so slow. Too slow for that lane. At 55 miles per hour, I was gaining on them from the inside lane. What the hell is this? There were two guys; one driving, the other in the shotgun seat. The driver was Michael Blodgett and the passenger was Robert Astin. You know that, of course."

"I do."

"At first I thought Blodgett was falling asleep. Then, another car quickly appeared behind them, fast. This driver, a young female, was going about 70, normal speed for the passing lane. Poor thing had to slam on her brakes or she would have rear-ended these guys. Then she flips on her high beams. I could almost read her lips, 'Move over, sap, you don't belong in this lane.'

"Blodgett doesn't budge.

"Meanwhile, I'm passing both vehicles from the slow lane. The girl, who had to be tired of waiting, pulls into the middle lane. She accelerates and passes from the middle lane, and then returns to the passing lane. I could tell it was a girl because of the light coming from the opposite direction. It created a silhouette of her, from shoulders up, highlighting her pony tail. She was alone."

"Much traffic?"

"Lots. Remember Dave, it's six in the evening on a Sunday, and we're twenty odd miles south of Boston."

"I can picture it."

"Well, picture this. When she made her pass and slipped back into the passing lane, Blodgett sped up and snuggled in close behind her. Tailgate close. And then the jerk flashes on his high beams.

"What the hell is this, I ask myself? What is this jackass doing? I look over and it seems like Blodgett and Astin are engaged, havin' fun. These road rogues are playing a game of cat and mouse. That's the deal here. They're blocking the high-speed lane to lure a motorist into giving them the high beams. The girl's initial high-beaming was the green flag signaling Blodgett to begin a pursuit of an innocent victim. It's like call and return in music, only there's deceit and malice in one of the players. And it's happening right under my nose.

"I'm appalled. That's just not right. Suppose that was my daughter? Supposing this guy gets the girl to pull over? Then what might happen?

"I kinda' lost my cool. I was so pissed off. I wondered, what can I do? My first reaction was to mind my own business. That's what most people would do. But is that the honorable thing to do? Momentarily, I had not a single idea. My teeth were grinding. I've always hated bullies. These bastards were bullies *and* predators. Then, in an instant, I knew. I'd give Michael Blodgett and his pal, Robert Astin, a taste of their own medicine.

"So I sped up and pulled into the passing lane, stationed myself directly behind them, and turned on *my* high beams, determined to bring this farce to an end. Resolved that intervention was appropriate."

"Kind of a ballsy thing to do?"

"Maybe. Hindsight is twenty-twenty vision. I don't know, Dave. Tell ya this, I felt an instant rush, a feeling of bizarre satisfaction, knowing the pursuer was to become the pursued."

"Really?"

He straightened his eyeglasses. "Absolutely. These fuckers deserved a taste of their own rotten medicine."

"You've already said that," I responded. "And, by the way, since when does a Baptist deacon use so many curse words?"

"Try spending over ten years in a slammer."

"OK. I'll leave that one alone."

"Where was I? Oh yes, my increase in speed woke Sandra up. 'Do you have your high beams on?' she asked me.

"'Yes I do.'

"'Why?'

"'Did you see what that man did?'

"'I was sleeping.'

"'This will be over in a minute.'

"I was now doing about 65 miles per hour. Nervous, yet alert, keeping a safe distance, maybe 100 to 200 feet behind. Maintaining my high beams. I explained to Sandra what happened, and she said, 'I don't like this. I'm very uncomfortable.'

"The pursuit continued for several miles. Then Blodgett slowed and I drew closer. I could see Astin's head come out of his window. He was a big guy. They were both big. Astin threw a bag of trash at us, just missing the windshield. We were startled. I allowed the distance between us to spread.

"About five minutes later, they suddenly accelerated and moved into the middle lane, rapidly separating distance. I looked over at Sandra, who exhaled. This madness was over with. I gained some degree of satisfaction knowing the innocent girl escaped unharmed.

"I could see them in the distance. We were both in the middle lane. Sandy and I were discussing the incident, unaware that Blodgett had dramatically reduced his speed without stepping on his brakes; so, there were no warning lights. I rapidly closed ranks. Then, Blodgett came to a complete stop."

"What?" I interrupted. "In the middle of Route 95?"

"Yes. Exactly, in the middle lane of the most highly traveled highway on the east coast."

"What the hell did you do?"

"What else could I do? I slammed on my brakes. They screeched. Sandra screamed. Traffic swerved and swayed all around us. Horns blowing. Fucking crazy. Especially when Blodgett threw a drink at us from his window. He leaned out and shook his fist. Big hulking guy, filled up the window.

"I experienced an adrenaline overload. My body trembled. I placed my right hand on my left arm, begging both to stop shaking. We sat for maybe a minute; seemed like an eternity. Madness had replaced an afternoon of fun. Finally, Blodgett got underway. Very slowly.

"Continuing to shake, I had difficulty shifting gears. I remember thinking, with certainty, that I must stay behind these maniacs, couldn't dare pass and give them the opportunity to sideswipe me or run me off the road. Another thing, I was at a disadvantage because of the lousy condition of my ten-year-old Toyota.

"Then Blodgett moved into the passing lane. I held my position in the middle lane, staying behind. We were going around 50 when Blodgett cut back into the middle lane and came to another complete stop."

"You gotta be kidding me."

"Wish I were. I couldn't believe it. At least I was better prepared. I stepped on and off my brake pedal, trying to warn traffic behind me. My tires screeched again. Again, traffic was forced to deke and maneuver around both vehicles. A will of God that no collision occurred. I could see Sandra clenching her fists in front of her chest. I continued to shake.

"And Blodgett just sat there.

"Somehow, as we waited in that Purgatory, I regained some composure. I had no choice but to stay calm. At least try to. We were still alive. I recall thinking Blodgett knew exactly what he was doing, as though he had the whole thing planned out. That he had done this before.

"Then he gets underway again, slowly, and moves into the inside lane. I follow. I must stay behind, cannot dare to pass. We're approaching the I-495 North exit. I realize that in a few more miles we'd be coming to the I-295 exit, which I normally take to Woonsocket. Maybe there'd be a chance to escape. But Blodgett pulls another uncanny move. He fakes an exit onto 495. Like a quarterback on wheels he veers toward the exit ramp. Then, at the last second, as I'm closing in behind him, he slips back into the inside lane, right in front of me, and continues south on 95."

"Why did he do that?"

"I'm not 100-percent sure. But I'd bet the family jewels they saw my Rhode Island plates and figured I'd continue south on 95. And that's surely what I would have done. Or, if he continued straight, I would have taken the 495 exit. So, he faked the exit. And it worked.

"For his final encore, Blodgett pulls into the breakdown lane and comes to a complete stop. Just like that. What's this move all about? What the hell is he doing now?

"I pull in behind him, keeping my distance, about 100 feet back." Don paused, eased back in his chair and folded his hands, as though we were in church. "Are you alright, David?"

"I think so. Yeh, absolutely. This is becoming a remake of *High Noon.*"

Weakly, we both smiled.

"So, I should go on?"

"Of course, no doubt. I'm taking copious mental notes."

"You're sure? It doesn't get any prettier."

"I know it doesn't, Don. Keep going, by all means."

He sat erect, adjusted his eyeglasses, and looked straight ahead. "OK. Sandy and I stayed glued to our seats, praying they'd cool off and drive away. At that moment I had no course of action, no ideas, other than to gain control from the shakes. I felt claustrophobic, like enclosed in a small, stalled elevator, thinkin' the cable's gonna' break, know what I mean?

"Sandy said, 'This is getting worse.' She stared out the window imploring them to leave. Not to be. The two of them exited their vehicle at the same time, advancing on ours, Blodgett on my side, Astin on Sandra's. Blodgett held one of those long, black police flashlights, a Maglight.

"I looked in my rear-view mirror. Should I make a dash for it? Could I get back on the highway? Not a chance. These two were pros at this, who cleverly timed their pull-over during a heavy traffic flow. Which, of course, prevented me from driving off. Now that I had pulled in, I was also boxed in.

"As I watched their deliberate, cadenced advance, I said to Sandra, 'We have big trouble coming down here.' After all, I weighed about a buck fifty back then, and these two guys looked like linemen for the New England Patriots.

"Sandra tried to respond. Nothing came out but dry fear. She looked forward and saw Astin some forty paces from her window.

"OK, remember, I'm an army veteran. I understand that moments like these precipitate what is known as the fight-or-flight response. Folks don't talk about the third response, paralysis, which I kinda' think is the rule rather than the exception. And that was Sandra's condition, through no fault of her own. Most haunting sight of my life.

"I wanted to run. That was my first impulse. But I couldn't. I'd be rammed by an oncoming car. I took one final peek at the highway, scanned everything, quickly. The roadside shoulder was illuminated like a golf driving range. I hoped a motorist might spot the problem and pull over. Maybe a state trooper.

"What could I do? I read the fear on Sandra's face, a helpless, frozen fear. I must defend her. I had a crossbow in the trunk. Can I get to it in time? I grabbed the keys from the ignition and ran to the back of the car. There's no way they could have missed seeing me. The frantic way in which I ran had to be a tip that I was up to something. Maybe it would scare them off. But no, they continued to advance, faster, closing in like a vise. Two against one.

"My trunk was disheveled from the two panic stops. But I had enough time to pull out the crossbow. Out of desperation. Out of nothing. Out of something, I managed to regain some composure. I said to myself, 'I'm not goin' down without a fight.'

"Try to picture this, David. I've got the weapon in my hand. I cock the crossbow from the right-shoulder-arms position. Then I back away from the car several steps, giving me a little more distance. I pull a bolt from the quiver. While I'm loading the bolt onto the bow, Blodgett and Astin arrive at the rear of my car. They're close, I'm tellin' ya, Blodgett advancing and Astin circling behind. I released the safety and positioned the weapon on my right hip. I warned them, 'Hold it right there.' They kept advancing. 'You'd better get back to your car.'

"Blodgett pointed that big flashlight into my eyes and shouted at me, 'What's your fuckin' problem, asshole?'

"I stepped back, worried that Astin might jump me from behind. I'm boxed in but good. I turned my head from the flashlight's bright glare. Once more, I told them to stop and go back. Blodgett yells again, 'What's your problem?'

"I could feel Astin behind me. Couldn't retreat. Couldn't see hardly at all. Blodgett's closing in. Things are moving very fast. He's within spitting range. He reaches out, and down, grabbing at the weapon still on my hip. This action brings pressure on the trigger. The bolt flies.

"At first, I thought it flew over his head." Donald squeezed his hand into a fist, unclenched it, rested it over his mouth, and talked through his hands. "Expected in milliseconds they'd be on me. Instead, silence. Then Blodgett yells, 'What the fuck?'

"From behind Astin asked, 'What's the matter?'

"'He shot me. There's an arrow in my shoulder. He must have more. Get his license number.'

"I see Astin moving from out of the darkness to my left and heading to my car. I backstep and reload the crossbow, regaining enough vision to see the bolt flopping in Blodgett's right shoulder. He didn't seem to be in pain, nor disabled; however, he did stop advancing. Then he stepped toward my car. I could see him reaching for his shoulder, twisting hard and ripping the arrow out. 'I've been shot. This mother-fucker shot me.'

"Blodgett pounded his flashlight into the left rear taillight of my car. Glass shattered everywhere.

"I knew Sandra was sitting in horror. I stayed put. For a split second, I'm eyeball to eyeball with Blodgett.

"Then they beat a retreat. The same way they came. They stopped in front of my car. They talked. I could see Sandra's shadowy form, in detail, sitting frozen and terrorized in the shotgun seat. Gotta be the most bizarre moment of my life. Our life. Think about it.

"At that point they headed back to their car. Astin helped Blodgett into the front passenger seat, then walked around to the driver's side. He paused, and took one last look back.

"I stood there rock-still, crossbow in hand. Watched them drive off. Went to my trunk, removed the bolt, set it in the trunk, and closed it. Then I ran like hell to Sandra.

"'Are you alright,' I asked?

"'I don't know. I think so. What just happened?'

"'I think I shot a man.'

"'You think?'

"'I was disoriented, Sandra. I don't remember firing the weapon.'"

Don looked at me from a retro-world of vivid visions. "Out of shock and fear, David, my mind must have blanked at the precise moment Blodgett reached out for the crossbow. For sure there was movement enough to create pressure on the trigger. I don't know if that makes any sense to you. All I can say is, to this day, I cannot perfectly recreate the moment of no return."

He continued, "I waited, looked around, everywhere, then got back on the highway. And to my amazement, driving south, we could not believe what we saw. There they were again, up ahead. Sandra said, 'Oh my God. What are they doing now?'

"They were poking along, probably discussing their next move. Astin was in no hurry, so I figured Blodgett was just winged by the arrow. Again, I stayed way back, out of harm's way.

"Astin pulled off 95 at the Route 152 / Attleboro exit.

"'They're gone,' Sandra nodded. The poor thing was trembling, tears ran down her face. 'I cannot believe what just happened. You shot one of them, Donald? Which one?'

"'The big guy.'"

"'They were both big.'

"'The driver. Definitely the driver. The other guy was behind me. It all happened so fast. I don't even remember getting off the shot, but it was the driver alright. The bolt caught his right shoulder. I saw the bolt.'

"'He must be OK. He made it to his car.'

"'I suppose so. It never should have gone that far.'

"'Well it did, Donald. The whole thing is terrible. Never should have happened. We must tell the authorities.'

"'Yes, I agree. The Woonsocket police? The state police?'

"'We're in the state of Massachusetts.'

"'Maybe we should call a lawyer?'

"'Maybe we should. But please, let's get home first. I'm sick. Then we'll figure out what's the best thing to do. My head is splitting. I just want to go home. I want to brush my teeth.'

"And that's what we did. Sandra was very pissed at me. I know she wanted to let me have it, but she held her thoughts. For the remainder of the ride, we rode mostly in silence. When we did talk, it was about who to call. The half hour it took to get home from the Attleboro exit seemed like an eternity, but we finally made it." Don frowned. "Hell of a day.

"As soon as we got home, Sandy ran right upstairs to the bathroom. I got the crossbow from the trunk and uncocked it. I was disgusted with the results. It was my experience that people backed away when they simply saw my crossbows. And remember, I used them only on targets. Neither of these guys behaved according to my expectations. I was also upset because the driver, Blodgett, had tried to disarm me, got himself winged, and had taken off with my sixteen-dollar, fancy-tipped arrow. The incident undermined my whole theory of home-defense. I kept two crossbows on the second floor in the bedroom, one crossbow on the first floor in the dining room, one crossbow in the basement's laundry room. I also had a harpoon on my living room wall. And believe me, you wouldn't want that in your gut. My self-defense theory is predicated on the fact that a crossbow loaded with a broad head is just as lethal as a handgun, and any armed intruder would take his business elsewhere when so confronted. I was angry because I found out I was wrong. The reason? I was dealing with psychopaths. And it dawned on me that many men become psychopaths in a fit of anger. I should have realized that, but I didn't.

"So, I decided to take the crossbow into the house and brought it down to the basement. When I came up to the kitchen, Sandy was coming down from upstairs, and we talked again about which police department to call. Both Stephen and Stuart [two of three sons] were home, upstairs, unaware of what had happened.

"While Sandy and I were talking, a Woonsocket cruiser pulled into our driveway, and two officers came to the back door. I opened the door and asked if they were here because of the crossbow shooting on I-95. My comment took them by surprise. They said they were. I stepped outside and closed the door and took them to my car to show them the taillight damage from Blodgett's flashlight. They asked to see the trunk and I opened it for them. They asked about the crossbow and I described it to them, and said it was in the house. I asked if they wanted me to get it. They did. It was my intention to get the weapon and bring it outside to them, as I didn't want them in my house. I had an extensive weapons collection and Stephen had a gun collection that included seventeen pieces.

"Unbeknownst to me, they followed behind and entered the kitchen with drawn pistols and ordered me to sit down at the kitchen table. Sandra told them to get out of her kitchen with those guns. They told her to sit down at the table. I can't remember their names. One officer asked if anyone else was in the house, and we told them we thought our sons were upstairs. One held us at gunpoint, while the other retrieved Stephen and Stuart at gunpoint. Then, one held us at gunpoint, while the other searched the house for weapons. They gathered all my crossbows and made a call to the Woonsocket police department.

"Lt. Jack Marzini arrived and the officers asked him if he had a consent-to-search form, and he said, 'No.' Sandy and I related our story about the Blodgett/Astin attack, and my defense. They used my phone to contact head-quarters. Then, we were arrested.

"At the Woonsocket police department Sandy and I each gave statements that were printed out for us to read and sign. Then Massachusetts troopers arrived and I was asked to sign a consent-to-search form, so they could examine my car. I did sign. Later, Sandy and I gave separate statements to the Massachusetts police. We did not sign them. We spent the rest of the night in unheated cells without blankets. Remember, this is February." Don looked at me and held up his hands, palms open. "And that, my friend, is the story."

"That's one hell of a story, Don. I am so sorry."

"Thank you, David." Don pointed his finger at me. "Listen here, here's an irony. On most Sundays we'd eat our dinner meal at home in Woonsocket around noontime. After class we'd head directly home. Had we not stopped at HoJo's, we would have gotten home much earlier. Blodgett and Astin would have been in a different time zone. Nonexistent. Talk about fucking fate. Instead, we ate dinner and pulled out of HoJo's around six."

I shook my head. I wanted to smoke another cigarette.

Don inhaled deeply. Catching his breath, he said, "Blodgett died about six hours later."

A prison guard's voice blared throughout the room instructing that all visitors must leave in five minutes. I looked at the clock on the prison wall. Three hours had passed. The wife dressed in the Islamic robe embraced her husband; the boy hugged his father's leg. Convict and wife exchanged a long, passionate kiss.

I snapped to attention. "Hey Don, I'm not gonna kiss you goodbye."

"That's quite alright."

We both smiled and stood. We shook hands. "This is an amazing story. I've got a million thoughts running through my mind."

"I bet you do."

"Appreciate you sharing it, Donald."

"Now you know."

"I'm home till January. I'll be back soon."

"Sure hope so. Thank you for coming up here, David. I'm grateful for that."

I watched Donald walk away. As he opened the last door, he looked back and gave me a nod. Hair rose on my arms.

Donald S. Graham at trial.   Michael D. Blodgett

On the dusky drive home surrounded by shadowy autumn scenery, I tried to remember highlights of our conversation. Somewhere within the context of our exchange I might discover a clue or an answer which could be submitted to an appellate attorney on Don's behalf. A move that might set my friend free. I could only focus on those two abrupt stops on Route 95; a miracle that Don didn't plow into Blodgett and Astin. How the hell did they all survive that scenario without a severe accident? Maybe Blodgett didn't come to a complete stop, he only slowed down. Maybe it was a figment of Don's imagination. I had difficulty with that one, and that's all I could focus on regarding our conversation. I couldn't hold another thought. My mind was a vacant sieve, as though some vertigoed, uninvited spirit had overwhelmed me and followed me from the prison to my car. Don's story blended and twisted its way through my memory and came out the other end like the remnants of a paper shredder. So, I drove in limbo with Don's voice zooming in and out of my mind, until it eventually faded away and was replaced by a memory of Maureen, my fiancée, and her brother, Jack.

It was the winter of 2005; eleven years after the tragedy. Maureen and I were living in San Francisco and Jack flew out for a short visit. On Jack's first day, we drove him all around town and ended up at Fisherman's Wharf, where we took a water taxi out to Alcatraz. Yeh, I'd forgotten all about that.

The guided tour was informative and held everyone's interest, even children. Fathers took family photos in front of prison cells, in the cells, ruefully warning their kids that they better be good or their destiny might be "The Rock." The crowd oohed and aahed when Al Capone's name was mentioned. The famed Chicago gangster was a bonafide "Rock" star, his mug featured on brochures and books in the gift shop.

Along the way, in one of the hallways, I shook hands with an Indian chief who was hawking his book about the Native American takeover of Alcatraz in the 60s. He was an animated, redfaced elder, short and roly-poly, and probably the only Indian who prospered from the entire campaign. Maureen was fascinated by the chief and she managed to chat with him at length. Later, still caught up in a verve, she lectured Jack and me about injustices, especially the plight of the Native Americans and the mistreatment of Alcatraz prisoners who had "no opportunity for rehabilitation."

Stored away in our Anchorage condo, I have a photo from that day. It's a comical shot of Jack inside one of the prison cells. He's plopped on top of a commode; a shit-eating grin spread across his face. I perfectly recall the moment. After taking the picture, he said with a dead serious face, "It's good to know that back in the day the 'worst of the worst' were held securely on this rock." I can still hear him laughing, "There's not much room in this cell, is there?"

I couldn't laugh. Not with the thought and vision of Donald lying on his tiny cot in the middle of the dark night, every night, replaying his fate, detail after detail, moment by moment.

Later, a half hour before we took the water taxi back, I was sitting outside, on concrete steps high up on an outer wall of the prison. Below were jagged rocks, then the Bay, and in the reachable distance stood the beautiful hills of San Francisco, fronted by the Piers, its skyscrapers, and higher still, roofs of opulent homes.

Like so many before me, I sat mesmerized, trying to imagine how anyone could escape The Rock. I could see how difficult it would be to negotiate the powerful Bay currents, the bitterly cold water, and the peril of sharks.

Soon, it got windy and cold, even with the sun still shining. I wondered how many inmates, throughout the years, sat on these very steps? Some in reverie, most in Purgatory. Others planning and plotting. Others sensing a kiss, an embrace from a lover who still lived in the city, so close, just a short swim away. Many a dream and fantasy had to be played out on these hard steps. Pacts with the Devil and God.

Chapter Two

Late February 1994

Major events of 1994:

- In a midterm election, the Republicans gain control of Congress.
- Nelson Mandela elected president of South Africa.
- Yasser Arafat, Palestinian Liberation Organization leader, along with Israel's Shimon Peres and Yitzhak Rabin, win Nobel Prize for peace.
- No World Series.
- Pulitzer Prize won by Edward Albee *(Three Tall Women)*.
- Oscar for Best Movie — *Forest Gump*.
- *Seinfeld* — hottest show on TV.

dea.con n. 1. A clergyman ranking just below a priest. 2. A lay assistant to a minister. [<Gk. diakonus, attendant.]

February 21, 1994 — 6:05am

While I was shaving, Dave Richards of Radio Station WWON announced Woonsocket's early edition of the news. All about Donald Graham.

"Holy shit." I stared into the mirror in disbelief.

"This is impossible," I shouted at the mirror, incapable of accepting the words and nearly nicking the mole on my chin. "This cannot be. Not Don! And poor Sandra, she must be beside herself."

At noon, in Floru's Restaurant on Main Street in Woonsocket, I sat with Vic Blank, a friend and business acquaintance since 1965, the same year, coincidentally, I ended my active duty in the navy and hung my shingle, *David G. Brown, A.A. Brown Insurance Agency.*

Even though he's ten years my senior, Vic and I are fast friends. We're compatible because of our vast differences. Vic has a photographic memory, while I wear out pencils taking notes. Vic's a math whiz. I still don't get fractions. He's a handy guy to have around. How I beat him at gin rummy remains a mystery. We're both big sports fans, especially when it comes to the Boston Red Sox. He hates them. I love them. However, we both ardently follow the trials and tribs of the New England Patriots.

Vic's a dead-serious kind of guy, a conscious person. He also owns the loudest sneeze on the east coast and possesses a contagious laugh. I've always taken to his sense of humor, which ranges from dry and witty to slapstick.

Today, there was nothing slapstick in Vic's voice. "Did you read the paper?"

"Did I. It's all about Donald Graham."

"It sure is. Not good publicity for Woonsocket. Soon, even burglars and thieves will be afraid to drive to Woonsocket." He smiled sardonically. "What a god-awful scene that must have been for the Grahams. What a confrontation. Two against one. And a crossbow. Can you believe it? How do these things happen?"

"It's beyond me. Just awful."

"You know Mr. Graham, right?"

"You know I do, Vic. Don's a client and a friend."

"I thought so. What kind of guy is this?"

"This is a good guy. If he was having lunch with us right now, we'd be talking hot-stove baseball."

"He's a killer."

"That's a pretty harsh judgement without the benefit of a trial."

"Maybe so. But regardless of the trial outcome, we know he let that arrow fly. There's blood on his hands."

"You're undeniably correct."

"So, why do you defend him?"

"It's an automatic. He's my friend."

"With all due respect, I don't know if that should be a criterion."

"Well, for me, it is. I cannot see Don Graham being a ruthless killer."

"There are probably people who think the same about Adolf Hitler."

"Come on now, Vic. Don's a good guy. A good husband, has three sons. He's religious and retired. He plays a mean game of cards. He's one of those serious, unilateral-thinking characters who has the ability to redeem his resolve with a dry, witty sense of humor." I pointed my finger. "He reminds me of you."

"OK, I'll admit that doesn't sound like a killer."

"Damn right."

"I remember you talking about him. On several occasions. Always favorable comments."

"Absolutely. Ya know, something stuck with me the first time I ever met Don, and I couldn't get a handle on it until right now."

"What's that?"

"Adaptability. That's it. I've never met a man who is so adaptable. That's not easy, ya know."

"Hey, I'm originally from New York, remember."

"I do, I do. Don and you are both outsiders. He grew up in New Brunswick, Canada and served in the United States Army. He worked in Massachusetts, and finally settled in Woonsocket, joined the First Baptist Church of Woonsocket and became deacon. The man adapts, I'm telling you. Even in a town like Woonsocket."

"Interesting," Vic said. "And let's face it, it's no Utopia. No one says, 'See Woonsocket and die.'"

Woonsocket is a world unto itself, located in the northeastern corner of the smallest state in the Union. It evolved into the center of the New England Industrial Revolution, and flourished in the textile industry. Several four-story, red brick factories are spread along the Blackstone River. They produced wools and yarns and clothing, three shifts a day, six days a week, year after year, until the early 1960s when factory owners began closing shop due to excessive utility and labor costs. Many moved south or out of the country altogether. My father wrote insurance policies for several of those mills.

The city has a distinct French-Canadian flavour highlighted by the use of their Canuck *patois.* The population of 50,000 is mostly from the Province of Quebec; migrants who came to work the mills. Before that the Narragansett, Ponagansett and Blackstone Indians ruled the roost, where salmon spawned in the soon-to-be-spoiled Blackstone River.

Edwin O'Connor hails from Woonsocket. In the mid-90s, he wrote *The Last Harrah,* a tale shadowing the career of Boston's infamous mayor, James Curley. Great musicians such as jazz pianist, Dave McKenna, and saxophonist, Greg Abate, are favorite sons. There are successful professional athletes, Clem Labine, Rocco Baldelli and Hall-of-Famer Napoleon Lajoie in baseball. Mathieu Schneider and Brian Berard in hockey, who both played for Mount Saint Charles Academy's hockey team that won 26 consecutive high school state championships. "The Mount" is located in the city.

Woonsocket was an "All-American City" when I was a kid in the mid-50s. You'd think we were elected to host the World's Fair. Signs everywhere; even a parade. During the city's heyday, a weekly ritual occurred on Thursday nights when downtown was flooded with shoppers "making their stores." Our entire family partook in the ritual. We'd shop at McCarthy's, Najarian's and Kornstein's. On the way home we'd stop at the Social Department Store, in the heart of "Social Queue," the French-Canadian District. Eddie Baram's father founded the Social Department Store. Mr. Baram was the first American retailer to use a layaway plan, and the locals loved it. Eddie and I have stayed close friends.

That entire era has faded, disappearing like Atlantis. I adored those times of closeness, unlocked doors, fresh-tasting tap water, balanced budgets, and meaningful handshakes. Back in those days, I could understand all the lyrics to all the music, and only Superman had blue hair.

When the factories started closing down, Woonsocket fell to hard times. The city became somewhat of a joke to the remainder of the state. We were out of favor, passe, "those Canuck leftovers up north." Most of my high school classmates left, seeking greater fortune. It's "leftovers" like Eddie Baram and me, along with fresh-blooded "outsiders" like Vic Blank and Don Graham, who stayed the course.

"Like I said, Vic, Donald Graham is adaptable. He's not your typical Woonsocket mill worker, nor a Flying Frenchman, but he sure fits into Woonsocket like a tight glove."

"How long have you known him?"

"Several years. When my father decided to go into semi-retirement seven years ago, he turned the Woonsocket Baptist Church account over to me. He said the contact person was Deacon Donald Graham. Deacon Don. So, about two months before the policies renewed I called Mr. Graham and set up an appointment at the church. I remember Don's first words after shaking my hand. 'Your father is a good man. Do the job he's done and you'll never lose our account.'

"I never did. As a matter of fact, in the late 1980s the Church had a water seepage loss that damaged their magnificent organ. I satisfactorily intervened in the settlement of that claim. Don was pleased, as were many of the parishioners. As a result, several gave me their insurance business, and Don was never hesitant to give me leads."

"Nice. That's how it's supposed to work. Isn't the *Because He Lives* ministry located at the church?"

"Yes it is. It's in the basement. Don Graham led me to *Because He Lives*. Introduced me to Paul Dempster, the ministry's founder, and we three went right to work assessing the insurance needs of this 'soup kitchen' ministry. Paul Dempster was a dynamo. If anyone was one of God's favorite children, it was Paul, with Donald pulling up the rear.

"Thinking back, having a working relationship with the likes of Paul and Donald was fun. I know that Don would do anything for the ministry. From the very beginning he welcomed Paul into the basement of his First Baptist Church. Along with Gil Perez, another deacon, he helped set up the kitchen, and acted as Paul's liaison to the church fathers."

"All good."

"Yes, all good. My father found good accounts."

"I miss your dad. And your mom. Al and Dolly Brown were quite the team."

"I miss them too, Vic. I think about them every day."

"You're a lucky guy, David."

"I am. I know. Actually, Dolly was the mixer, she would have made a terrific insurance agent."

"I agree, but in that generation the Dolly Browns of the world stayed home with the kids."

"Yup."

"Your father had a wonderfully dry wit. I can picture Al. His tongue always stuck out when he laughed."

"Yes it did. Can you picture his hair style? When I was a kid I'd watch him in the bathroom apply a dose of Slickum to his scalp. An orange, adhesive goo that shined and fused his hair from front to back like Clark Kent's."

"Guess he did that so his hat wouldn't mess up his hair?"

"Never thought of that."

"So it was Al who brought you Donald Graham?"

"He sure did."

"None of what you're talking about sounds like the lead-in to a murder case."

"I know."

Donald and Sandra Graham at home (1992)

Donald S. Graham was born on April 30, 1939 at the Victoria Hospital in Fredericton, New Brunswick, Canada.

His early years were shaped during World War II. Many of his relatives served in the Canadian navy and air force. His uncle, Robert Adamson, was killed while flying in a Lancaster bomber over Germany in 1940. On Queen Street in downtown Fredericton there's an officers' barracks from the 18th century that has been converted into a military museum and contains a list of the New Brunswick war dead from both World Wars. Only the Gordon family sacrificed more members than the Grahams. Coincidentally, in Edinburgh, a list reveals that more Scottish Gordons died than Grahams during the two wars.

Providence Journal article dated February 22, 1994:

Church Deacon, 54, charged in Route 95 crossbow killing

First came an argument on the road.
Then the drivers faced off. <u>There were words</u> ... and a bolt from a crossbow slammed onto one man's chest.

By Jonathan Saltzman & Paul Edward Parker
Journal-Bulletin Staff Writers

It started early Sunday evening, as a duel of flashing high beams in the passing lane on Route 95 in Mansfield, Mass.

It ended with an ambulance attendant from Attleboro, Mass., getting shot in the chest with a crossbow, and a church deacon from Woonsocket and his school secretary wife facing charges in his slaying.

Michael Blodgett, 42, an attendant for Brewster Ambulance Service of Boston, was heading home from his day-shift with a fellow worker about 6:30 p.m., when he flashed his high beams to pass a motorist, according to John Letourneau, an assistant district attorney in Bristol County.

He wasn't the only driver in a hurry. Donald S. Graham, 54, of Woonsocket was heading south as well, returning with his wife, Sandra, 51, from their Sunday afternoon ritual of ballroom dancing in the Attleboro area. He was driving behind Blodgett and flashed his high beams to pass.

Eventually, both Blodgett and Graham pulled into the breakdown lane on a stretch of darkened highway in Mansfield, just north of North Attleboro. Police will not say what prompted both drivers to stop.

Words were exchanged. Then, police say, Donald Graham, a deacon and bookkeeper at the First Baptist Church in Woonsocket, reached into the trunk of his 1984 Toyota Cressida, withdrew a Barnett crossbow and shot Blodgett in the chest with a 16-inch bolt.

Graham got back into his car and drove home with his wife.

Blodgett's passenger, identified by police as Rob Astin, drove his bleeding friend to Sturdy Memorial Hospital in Attleboro. Blodgett was flown to the University of Massachusetts Medical Center in Worcester.

At 12:19 a.m. yesterday, less than six hours after the shooting, he was pronounced dead.

The Grahams, traced through the license plate number provided by Astin, were arrested at their two-story house at 619 Manville Rd., by Woonsocket police about 8 p.m. Sunday. Police seized five crossbows, including the one used in the shooting which, [said] family Court Judge Edward C. Clifton in Providence, where they waived their rights to an extradition hearing. *(sic)*

When Clifton asked Donald Graham whether anyone had threatened him into waiving his rights, the wiry Army veteran took a breath and answered in a reedy voice:

"Not to my immediate recollection. It's been a long day."

In response to a shouted question from reporters as he was led from the courthouse, Graham said, "It's the worse thing I ever did."

The Grahams were taken into custody by Massachusetts state police, and will be arraigned today in District Court, Attleboro.

Donald Graham, 54, a retired auto worker at the former General Motors factory in Framingham, Mass., faces a charge of murder. Sandra Graham, 51, a longtime secretary at Woonsocket High School, faces a charge of being an accessory after the fact.

During a break in the hearing yesterday, one of the Grahams' three sons came to his parents' defense and gave reporters a version of what happened Sunday night.

Stephen, 27, who was present when police interviewed his parents in their kitchen, said his father told police that Blodgett deliberately slowed his car to a crawl to prevent him from passing. His father also told police that Blodgett or the passenger in the car threw trash at his parents' moving car.

When the cars pulled off the highway, Stephen Graham said, the two men in Blodgett's car approached his father menacingly, one carrying a flashlight. Donald Graham loaded the crossbow and exhorted Blodgett to stop, Stephen Graham said.

"He told him, 'Stop. Stop. Don't come any closer!'" Stephen Graham said tearfully. "And they kept coming at him, and (the crossbow) just went off by *accident.* It's just unfortunate that he got the guy point-blank in the chest. It's too bad he didn't shoot him in the leg."

Stephen Graham, a field service technician for a medical laser company in Wayland, Mass., said his father is not a violent man and spends most of his time going over financial records on his personal computer, baking cookies and raising 11 Himalayan, Siamese and domestic cats. Donald Graham uses the crossbows for target practice, his son said.

Stephen Graham said his father should not have left the scene and driven home. But, he said, his father did not think he had seriously wounded Blodgett.

Blodgett's family "probably think my father's some maniac who goes around plugging people with a crossbow, but it's 180 degrees around," Stephen Graham said.

Support also came from the pastor of First Baptist Church in Woonsocket, who attended the District Court hearing, too. The Rev. Roger H. Francis said Donald Graham would not have shot Blodgett unless provoked.

"I don't see Donald behaving that way unless he was threatened," said Mr. Francis, who has known him for four years. He did say Donald Graham has a temper, however, "He feels strongly about injustice, anyone whose rights are not respected," he said.

A niece of Blodgett relays a different story from Astin.

The woman, who identified herself only as Stacy, said her uncle did nothing to threaten the Grahams. In fact, she said, Blodgett frantically tried to let Graham pass.

"Blodgett did everything he could to get Graham to pass him," she said in a telephone interview after speaking with Astin. "He sped up, slowed down and changed lanes," she said, "but Graham would not quit following."

She said Blodgett eventually pulled over into the breakdown lane because he thought someone in the Graham car had seen the emergency medical technician sticker on his car and needed help.

"There's no way he would antagonize anybody," she said, speaking from the house of Blodgett's brother, Edwin, of Attleboro. "He thought something might have been wrong."

"He got out of his mouth, 'Have you got a problem?' and the guy had a crossbow and shot him," the niece said.

Blodgett was divorced and had two sons, Michael, 13, and David, 6 months, his niece said.

Last night, Blodgett's grieving co-workers held a news conference at the Boston headquarters of Brewster Ambulance to decry his slaying. Blodgett, an emergency medical technician for 16 years, had worked at Brewster since June 1992.

"This country had better get some resolve in dealing with violence," said David Ladd, general manager. "This is just another example of people choosing a violent act to resolve whatever."

Bill Fennessy, senior operations manager, said Blodgett was a caring person who would help anyone.

"When is the violence going to stop?" he said. "I don't know what it's going to take, but it's got to stop somewhere."

Frank S. Graham, Donald's father, grew up in Keswick, New Brunswick, located along the St. Johns River. He was a farmer and hunter, earning a reputation as one of the Province's ace deer hunting guides. He also worked as a lumberjack. After marrying Elva Adamson, he became a mechanic and surveyor. His Achilles heel was alcoholism and he managed to disguise his addiction from his children.

The Grahams lived at 304 Charlotte Street in Fredericton. A few houses down the street near Windsor Park lived the O'Rees. Two of their sons, Sam and Willie, were archers. Donald was impressed with their marksmanship and received a bow and arrow for his thirteenth birthday. In the early 60s Willie O'Ree became the first black hockey player in the National Hockey League.

Below are February 23, 1994 *Providence Journal* excerpts:

Divergent views presented of crossbow assailant.

By Paul Edward Parker
Journal-Bulletin Staff Writer

ATTLEBORO, Mass. — Was Donald S. Graham of Woonsocket a self-appointed "guardian of the highways" or a man fearing for his life...

Those were the conflicting views lawyers presented to District Court Judge John J. Dolan yesterday when Graham and his wife, Sandra, were arraigned in the slaying of Michael Blodgett, 42, of Attleboro.

Prosecutor John Letourneau told the judge that Graham, 54, of 619 Manville Road, "took it upon himself to be the guardian of the highways," and he asked the court to set bail for him at $50,000 cash.

Defense lawyer David A. Cooper of Providence portrayed Blodgett and his passenger, Rob Astin of Attleboro — who worked together at a Boston ambulance service — as menaces who had backed Graham into a corner when the crossbow accidentally released its fatal shot.

"They were looking for trouble, and unfortunately they found it," Cooper said. He asked the court to set bail for Graham at $10,000 cash.

Judge Dolan set bail at $50,000 cash for Donald Graham and released Sandra Graham on her own recognizance.

Graham stood with his mouth open as Letourneau described the state's account of Sunday evening: Blodgett and Astin were heading home from work in South Boston when Blodgett flashed his high beams at a car in front of him.

Graham saw the beams flash and "apparently did not like that behavior," Letourneau said. Graham drew close to Blodgett and flashed his own high beams but did not pass, even though Blodgett gave him ample opportunity.

"He followed the victim for three or four miles," Letourneau said.

Then, Blodgett pulled over and stopped in the breakdown lane near the Mansfield–North Attleboro line, and Graham stopped behind him. Blodgett got out of his car, about 100 feet from the Grahams, and walked toward them.

Letourneau said Graham could have chosen to drive off then.

Instead, he got out, went to the trunk, took out his Barnett crossbow, cocked it, loaded a 16-inch bolt and shot Blodgett in the chest, Letourneau said.

Then, Letourneau said, Graham did several things that were "admissions of guilt": He drove home instead of going to the police. He removed the crossbow from the car and stored it in his house. He removed several arrows clipped to the bow and hid them.

When police arrived at his home, Graham admitted the shooting and led officers to the weapon. "This defendant pointed out the particular crossbow to the police and said, 'This is the crossbow I used,'" Letourneau said.

Graham stood with his head bowed, looking up only occasionally, as Cooper, his lawyer, described a much different scene:

Graham had tried repeatedly to get by Blodgett, but the other driver frustrated his every attempt, speeding up, slowing down, changing lanes, even throwing trash and ice from a cup of soda at the Grahams's car, Cooper said.

When Blodgett pulled into the breakdown lane, Graham stopped 100 feet behind him because he was fearful Blodgett would force his car off the road if he continued, Cooper said.

Blodgett and Astin got out of their vehicle and headed to the Grahams.

"They moved quickly in his direction," Cooper said. "My client went to the trunk and got some protection."

Graham intended to use the crossbow only to scare Blodgett and Astin off, Cooper said. Graham backed up until he was 30 feet behind his own car.

He stopped there, fearful for the safety of his wife in the car, Cooper said. "I think most people would agree at some point he's (Graham's) got to hold his ground. Blodgett walked up to arms reach ... at which point the bow discharged and went off," Cooper said.

The Grahams drove home because Blodgett and Astin had driven off, Cooper said. (Astin drove Blodgett to Sturdy Memorial Hospital, in Attleboro. He was later flown to the University of Massachusetts Medical Center, where he died. Astin gave police Graham's registration number, which they traced.)

When officers arrived at Graham's door, "he and his wife were home contemplating calling the police," Cooper said. "He took the police down to where the crossbow was."

A psychologist for the state, Charlotte Denton, examined Graham in the courthouse yesterday. She told Judge Dolan, "I see no reason to question his competency to stand trial."

Later, outside the courtroom, Cooper said he had not considered an insanity defense but could not rule it out.

"We intend to go to trial and be exonerated," Cooper said.

I could not picture Donald as a one-man posse acting as a "guardian." No, that's a bad description. The Charles Bronson *Death Wish* type character he is not. Furthermore, time is an element in the definition of guardian; like a librarian, who every day, for many years, "guards" the books.

Alarm spread it's harrowing tentacles over the entire congregation of the First Baptist Church of Woonsocket. Donald Graham, good friend and deacon, would be tried for murder! Impossible. Preposterous.

February 24, 1994 — Today's *Woonsocket Call* headline:

Crossbow suspect's bail bid rejected

NEW BEDFORD — A judge yesterday denied a bail reduction request from Donald S. Graham, 54, of Woonsocket, who is accused of killing a motorist with a crossbow after a traffic dispute on Interstate 95.

Graham, of 619 Manville Road, appeared before New Bedford Superior Court Judge Walter Steele. His attorney, David A. Cooper of Providence, asked the judge to reduce Graham's bail, which was set at $500,000 surety or $50,000 cash.

Steele refused.

Below are additional excerpts:

According to court records, Graham has a Massachusetts driver's license, but lost his Rhode Island license 25 years ago.

His Rhode Island license was suspended in 1969 after he was convicted in Massachusetts for drunken driving and for operating to endanger, according to published reports.

His Rhode Island license was never reinstated.

Graham continued to drive and was convicted of motor vehicle offenses in both states in the 1970s and the 1980s, including driving without a valid license, driving while intoxicated, speeding and leaving the scene of an accident, according to records at the Rhode Island Administrative Adjudication Court.

"He shouldn't have been behind the wheel," Robert Halpin, deputy administrator of Rhode Island's adjudication court said.

Graham obtained a Massachusetts driver's license at some point and told motor vehicle officials last year that he lived in Dedham, Mass., said Aubrey Hazner, a spokesman for the Massachusetts Registry of Motor Vehicles.

The article concluded:

Mrs. Graham was released Monday on personal recognizance, and was ordered to reappear in court on March 22.

Chapter Three

The Trial

In 1950 when Donald Graham was ten years old, his mother died of a thyroid condition. On the day of her passing, his father, Frank, was surveying a road in Newfoundland. Donald moved to Moncton, New Brunswick, to live with his aunt and uncle, Agnes and Edward Smith.

From ninth through the twelfth grade he attended Petitcodiac Regional High School. His principal, Colin Barrett, had Donald in physical education and English for three years. "Donald was an eager and affable honor student. Friendly, happy and talkative; his congenial disposition found favour with both fellow students and teachers. He stood out in many ways as a student with high aptitude and a myriad of interests, and took part in many extra-curricular activities."

He played varsity basketball, was a Petitcodiac Air Cadet, won the Best Actor award as Wilbur in the comedy, Love Hits Wilbur, *and was voted president of his senior class. To make a few extra dollars, he sold magazines. In June of 1957 Donald S. Graham graduated valedictorian of his class.*

July 9, 1995 — In his article, "Crossbow suspect released on bail," Russ Olivo, staff writer for *The Woonsocket Call*, wrote:

"I'm relieved is about all I can say," Graham said, in a brief telephone interview with The Call. "I was treated well, but the fact of the matter is incarceration isn't a very pleasant experience."

Graham is facing charges of murder, assault with intent to commit murder, driving to endanger and assault and battery by means of a dangerous weapon.

Graham's wife, Sandra, 51, who sat in the car with the windows rolled up and the doors locked during the shooting incident, was charged with being an accessory after the fact of assault and battery with intent to commit murder.

The Grahams are both expected to appear for preliminary hearings in District Court, Attleboro, on March 22. Lutes said he expects the State to dismiss the charges against Mrs. Graham, a 32-year employee of the Woonsocket Education Department.

While Assistant District Attorney John Letourneau said earlier this week the State has a strong case of first-degree murder against Graham, Lutes said his client did not instigate the confrontation and was not the chief aggressor. During Graham's arraignment Tuesday, Lutes and co-counsel David Cooper argued that a cup of ice and trash were thrown from the Blodgett vehicle onto Graham's car, and that the only reason Graham stopped behind Blodgett's car was because he did not want them following his vehicle.

The defense attorneys told Judge Dolan that Graham stopped his car 100 feet behind Blodgett's and that when the two men began walking toward him, Graham retreated another 30 feet behind his own car, ordering the men to stop before he fired the weapon.

Graham, who was arrested at his home early Monday morning, told police that he was not sure whether he pulled the trigger of the crossbow "intentionally or instinctively." But in court on Tuesday, Graham pleaded innocent, and his attorney said his weapon discharged accidentally.

Prosecutors said Graham used an arrow — bolt is actually the technical term for crossbow ammunition — that is specially designed to expand on impact and cause more bodily damage. Police seized five crossbows, including one Graham pointed out as the one he used to shoot Blodgett, plus an assortment of arrows, during a search of Graham's home.

On June 1, 1959 at the age of 20, Donald looked for employment in the United States. He was sponsored by his aunt and uncle, Claire and Donald Adamson, and lived with them in Needham, MA. There, he became a lab technician for the Ludlow Corporation.

During the summer of 1961 he met Sandra Thibault in Falmouth, Massachusetts, on the shore of Cape Cod. Sandra brought Don home the next day, a Sunday, to meet her parents. That night, they went to a drive-in to see Never on Sunday. *They were married in Newton, Massachusetts on November 20, 1961 by Monte Basbar, a Justice of the Peace. Donald was inducted into the army the next day.*

July 10, 1995

So warm today I worked up a sweat walking the two city blocks of Main Street, from my office to Floru's Restaurant. A quiet day. All the mills were closed. Most folks were on vacation. Vic Blank was already at a table when I arrived.

"I'm not happy with all this trigger talk about intentional, instinctive and accidental," I said. "Donald's defense should take that issue up during the trial, maybe while they're emotionally explaining his fight or flight response."

"I agree with that," Vic responded.

"Poor Sandra Graham. She's been charged with felonious crimes, as an accessory to assault and battery..."

"With intent to commit murder." Vic completed my sentence.

"Yes. This is a high school principal's assistant, as well as a deacon of her church. Can you imagine. To me it's incomprehensible."

"I didn't know both Grahams were deacons."

A Woonsocket lawyer friend was sitting at the table next to us and overheard our conversation. He walked over and pointed at his copy of *The Providence Journal.* "Seems like your boy will be OK."

"Glad you see it that way, counselor," I replied.

"Well, he's out on the streets. I don't condone what he did. But, what the hell, his wife was in the car. There's a lot to this story and some of it bodes well for Graham. My guess is he'll get manslaughter. He may have to serve time. Probably a short stay."

"Any chance for murder one?" I asked.

"Unlikely, but you never know. Massachusetts is of uncommon wealth!"

"That's not very funny. What the hell are you talking about?" Vic asked.

"Shit happens."

"That's one hell of an explanation."

"When it comes to practicing in Massachusetts, you must pay close attention because their laws are often times different. They have some cockeyed, antiquated statutes. Who knows, one could pop up and bite Donald Graham in the ass."

"For example."

"Hey, I gotta get back to work. Any more questions and I'll have to send you a bill."

(I intentionally failed to mention the lawyer's name because I never liked the guy. Always thought he was a typical legal shyster and was disappointed he overheard Vic and my conversation. Didn't realize we were talking that loud. Actually this guy has bionic ears and is probably accustomed to eavesdropping on people. At least his comments were favorable.)

Because he was a Canadian citizen, Graham registered for the draft to obtain "permanent resident alien" status. He served basic training at Fort Dix, New Jersey. He also enrolled in a sixteen-week course to qualify for marriage into the Catholic Church. Before reporting to Fort Bennings, Georgia for flight school, they remarried at Sandra's church in April of 1962. Paul Hamrock, a friend from basic training, was Donald's best man.

Almost fifteen months after the incident, the trial of the Commonwealth of Massachusetts vs Donald S. Graham was scheduled to begin on July 10, 1995 in the historic, ornate, red brick Bristol County Superior Court building located in New Bedford. At first glance this edifice looks more like a castle than a courthouse. It only lacks a moat.

New Bedford is an old whaling town that drew a steady import of tourists, but of late has lost attraction due to news of a harbor polluted with PCBs and a highly-publicized raping on a pool table at Big Dan's Cafe. Now, it will be the venue where Donald's fate will be decided if they ever get the trial underway.

Seems that the prosecuting attorney, Assistant Attorney General John Letourneau, managed to convince Judge Walter Steele to postpone because "some of his witnesses will be on vacation." Letourneau has a list of 20 potential witnesses (the defense has only submitted four names). Letourneau told the judge he'd provide affidavits to support his request. A displeased Steele, according to a quote in *The Woonsocket Call,* told Letourneau he should have known better than to schedule a murder case in July or August. "I don't want to read affidavits. I want to know when you're ready," Steele apologized to the defense counsels, David Cooper and Scott Lutes for the delay.

On the courthouse steps, *Woonsocket Call* reporter Russ Olivo quoted Donald as saying, "Prison, I've been there before (for a DUI charge in the 60s). I spent four days there. I almost gave up smoking. No, I'm not concerned about going to prison because I'm not going."

This brash comment hardly sounds like the Donald Graham I know. I can only think the pressure is mounting and Donald wants to project a positive attitude. I don't know; I don't like it.

From the Blodgett contingency, the victim's sister-in-law, Linda Blodgett, was quoted in *The Call*, "He's (Graham) going to do anything to make himself look good. Michael was a helper, not a destroyer. He wouldn't get involved unless he had to."

The victim's brother said he was anxious for the trial to begin so his brother's story could be told. He felt, to this point, the press was favoring Graham. Graham's side felt just the opposite, displeased that Prosecuting Attorney Letourneau was vilifying Donald.

As amateur criminal lawyers, the Floru lunch gang tried to understand why the defense counsel only had four witnesses. Made me think they were playwriting a sequel to *My Cousin Vinny,* instead of rounding up the best possible witnesses for a hard-ass murder trial. We also had trouble with the chronology of the court proceedings. The incident occurred on February 20, 1994 and here it is July 10, 1995, almost fifteen months later. Isn't that a long time between occurrence and trial?

Many of us became suspicious of Prosecutor Letourneau's request to delay based on witness problems. That seemed like a lame excuse. Maybe something else went wrong. Then, from out of the blue, Judge James McHugh replaced Judge Walter Steele. Why?

In October, 1962 Graham spent a tension-filled five days sitting beside the lead C-130 cargo plane scheduled to go to Cuba. By now he was a member of the elite 101st Airborne Division, immortalized by author John Ambrose. The 101st was the first military unit to be placed on DEFCON-2 status. They were not allowed to enter the aircraft during this waiting period, as to do so would set off the wrong signals to the rest of the Division. He had no idea what weapon loads were aboard.

October 31, 1995

Finally, the trial got underway in the courtroom of Judge James McHugh. Hell of a way to celebrate Halloween. The entire congregation of the First Baptist Church of Woonsocket and most of the Woonsocket community sat on the edge of their seats. I'm sure that held true for most of the residents of Attleboro. Actually, the case was gaining national notoriety. ABC's newsmagazine *20/20* was expected to begin taping trial segments for a program about highway violence, which had become known as *road rage*.

Indeed, the trail was hot. Like a classic tempest the media spread their tentacles cross country about an alleged statement from Donald saying he doesn't know if he pulled the trigger "intentionally or instinctively."

The first day-and-a-half was spent selecting the jury. The entire first day was conducted in closed quarters, Judge McHugh's office, with only Donald and the lawyers in attendance. Four of the twelve jurors were selected. Because a *Providence Journal* reporter complained, the trial was continued in open court on day two to its conclusion. I don't know why Donald's lawyers didn't object to this day-one process.

The closest Graham came to a war was when he trained for a tactical nuclear exchange to prevent a Soviet invasion into Germany. We know so much more now than we did back then. But, during the 60s, fear of another world conflict seemed very real. Dean Rusk was quoted as saying, "The Russians blinked (first)."

Thirty-three-year-old Robert A. Astin took the stand — Michael Blodgett's coworker at Brewster Ambulance Service in Boston and driving companion on the fatal night of February 20, 1994. Astin certainly qualified as one of Letourneau's key witnesses.

Here are excerpts from the November 4, 1995 issue of *The Woonsocket Call* as reported by staff writer, Russ Olivo:

Astin said he suspected trouble might loom if Blodgett pulled over, and warned against it. But Blodgett finally grew frustrated and stopped in Mansfield, saying, "This guy's a so-and-so. I'm going to pull over and ask him what his problem is."

Prosecutors say the other driver, Donald S. Graham, 56, a Woonsocket church deacon they have portrayed as a "guardian of the highway," murdered the 42-year-old EMT in an act of unprovoked retaliation for having seen Blodgett flash his high beams at a third motorist. But the defense says Graham acted in self-defense, a claim which Astin refuted in often testy exchanges with Graham's lawyer yesterday.

Under questioning by Assistant District Attorney John Letourneau, Astin said that after Blodgett pulled over, Graham stopped a couple of car lengths behind them and went to the rear of his vehicle.

Blodgett and he began approaching Graham's vehicle, Astin on the passenger side and Blodgett on the driver's side. As they neared Graham, Blodgett remarked, "What the hell do you think you're doing," said Astin. But he never got a chance to say anything else.

"I could see [Graham] holding something," said Astin. "I thought, 'Does he have a gun?' Then I thought it couldn't be. It was too wide.

"That moment seems frozen in time," Astin continued. "The three of us ...

Mike stopped, I stopped, Mr. Graham was standing there. I heard a noise, like an air noise. Mike said, "That blankety-blank. He shot me."

Graham, said Astin, flatly contradicting the defense's claims that the defendant warned Blodgett to keep away, "never said a word."

Astin initially didn't realize Blodgett had been shot with an arrow because it was too dark out. And Blodgett didn't seem that badly hurt, he said. Astin said Blodgett just seemed "mad" that he had been shot, calling out for his trauma bag in the car.

But as they were walking back toward their car, Blodgett collapsed. Astin said he went over to grab him by the shoulders and saw the arrow for the first time. Blodgett, he said, was soaked in blood. Astin jostled Blodgett into the car and drove as fast as he could to the nearest hospital, Sturdy Memorial in Attleboro, holding a spare T-shirt against his friend's wound on the way.

Astin said he never connected an earlier incident in which Blodgett had flashed his high beams at another motorist who sped off as being the reason for Graham to start chasing them.

Under cross-examination by defense counsel David A. Cooper, Astin tersely rebuked the attorney's suggestions that Blodgett and he wanted to attack Graham. At one point, Astin accused Cooper of lying.

Asked whether he hadn't previously told police he accompanied Blodgett to confront Graham because he wanted to protect his friend, Astin conceded he thought Blodgett was "a naive person" and that he "knew there was going to be a problem."

"I might have said I was afraid Mike was going to get his butt kicked," Astin said. "When somebody hounds you going down the highway that many miles, chasing you every time you change lanes, obviously they're not friendly. And yes, I may have said when Mike got out of the car, I was afraid he was going to get his butt kicked, and I might get my butt kicked just for being there."

Astin had said under questioning by the prosecutor that Blodgett slowed down once while Graham was chasing him in order to send him a message that he didn't like what Graham was doing. But under questioning by Cooper, Astin flatly denied that Blodgett had slammed his brakes on a second time, or that in either case, it was intended to force Graham to rear-end Blodgett's car.

Astin denied several key elements of Cooper's self-defense theory, among them, that Blodgett swore repeatedly at Graham; that he and Blodgett threw debris at Graham's car before the encounter; and that Blodgett made a lunge toward Graham before he was shot.

Regarding the latter, Astin told Cooper, "That's a lie, sir, a total lie."

Astin told Cooper he didn't remember Blodgett carrying a flashlight during the confrontation, although he said he might have told police previously he had done so.

The bolt which killed Blodgett was equipped with double razors which fan out on impact. Yesterday, the man who holds the patent on the bolt tip testified it was designed for hunting big game and to make it easier for hunters to track prey by letting a lot of blood.

The "Punchcutter" tip, as he branded it, is for hunting "bear, elk, antelope and deer," said Paul DeLucia, chief officer of Finished Archery Technology in Hopewell Junction, N.Y. He said the tip is designed to "promote rapid bleeding and blood trail for proper harvesting of game..."

Graham was discharged from the army on November 20, 1963 and returned to Massachusetts on November 23, 1963. Sandra and he stopped for lunch at the International House of Pancakes off Route 95 in Sharon, Massachusetts, where they learned that John F. Kennedy had been assassinated.

Russ Olivo's *Woonsocket Call* articles on November 7 and November 8, 1995 contained the following testimony from a Woonsocket policeman:

NEW BEDFORD, MASS. — When Woonsocket Patrolman T. Michael Cahill went to Donald S. Graham's house the night of Feb. 20, 1994, he wasn't sure Graham was the man Bay State authorities suspected of shooting an Attleboro EMT with a crossbow on Route 95 minutes earlier.

But that changed as soon as the Woonsocket church deacon answered the door of his home.

"You must be here about what happened on 95," Cahill recalled Graham saying as he testified on the third day of Graham's Superior Court trial for the murder of Michael Blodgett, 42.

Cahill was one of several police officers who testified Graham freely admitted shooting Blodgett, coolly describing the incident as the culmination of a highway chase he initiated to retaliate for Blodgett's flashing his high beams at another motorist.

Prosecutors portray Graham, 56, of 619 Manville Road, as an avenging "guardian of the highways" who embarked on a "chase of death" to repay Blodgett's discourteous roadside manner to a complete stranger. Charged with first-degree murder, he contends he acted in self-defense.

Under questioning by Assistant District Attorney John Letourneau, Cahill read a police statement in which Graham told him that he and his wife Sandra, a Woonsocket school secretary, had just come from a night of dance lessons in Canton when they saw Blodgett's car, in front of them, flash its high beams at another car.

Graham said he wanted to treat Blodgett "in like kind." With his high beams on, Graham told police he followed Blodgett the first time when he moved from the passing lane to the middle lane. When Blodgett moved from the middle lane to the passing lane, Graham said, he stayed put but didn't pass.

Blodgett then moved back into the middle lane, then the breakdown lane according to the testimony.

During the pursuit, Graham said a paper bag and a cup of ice were thrown from Blodgett's car into his path. And Blodgett twice slammed on his brakes. The second brake incident led Graham to end the pursuit and turn off his high beams, he said.

But when Blodgett finally pulled into the breakdown lane, "I did not want this car to follow behind me so I also pulled into the breakdown lane..." Graham told Cahill.

Graham said he realized "I had a problem" when he saw Blodgett carrying a flashlight. Graham told Cahill he knew he had a crossbow in the trunk and immediately went to get it as Blodgett and another man (Robert Astin), a passenger in Blodgett's car, began approaching him.

"Both people in the car got out at the same time and approached my car," said Graham. "The driver had a flashlight in his hand. I got out of my car and went to my trunk. I got out my crossbow and I cocked it. The people kept approaching me. I retreated and told them to stop. They kept coming.

"I had retreated about two car lengths behind my car and he was about arm's length away from me when I fired the weapon. I am not sure whether I intentionally pulled the trigger or instinctively pulled the trigger."

Cahill and another police witness yesterday said Graham told them he drove with a crossbow because he had heard a story of a woman who was stabbed by a drunk and he realized "he couldn't do much" to stop something like that.

Graham told Cahill that after the shooting he went home and put the Barnett Reverse Curve Bow in a basement cabinet, removing the usually-attached bolts. Four other crossbows were seized in other parts of the house with the ammunition attached. Graham showed police where they were, Cahill said.

Graham told Cahill that after the shooting Blodgett smashed the taillight of his car with his flashlight. Cahill said he checked the car and the taillight was indeed broken.

As Graham explained to Cahill how the expanding razor tip of the bolt used in the shooting worked, Cahill, under cross examination by defense counsel Scott Lutes, said Graham's demeanor was "very calm... He didn't appear to be anything."

As Massachusetts State Trooper Ronald Blais finished taking a similar statement from Graham at Woonsocket headquarters later that night, Graham spontaneously remarked, "I guess I just met a moron who wouldn't give up," Blais testified.

"He stated that he told the person to hold it... He said that twice. He said he saw the flashlight... Mr. Graham said (it) was used as a flashlight, not a weapon," said Blais.

"Did Mr. Graham indicate to you he fired the crossbow in fear?" asked David Cooper, another of Graham's lawyers.

"Yes he did," said Blais.

"It was my observation that Mr. Graham was very cool, calm, and collected during the entire interview," said Massachusetts State Trooper Denise Adams.

Many details of the incident contradict that of the state's key witness, Astin, who said Graham pursued Blodgett through at least seven lane changes and shot Blodgett without a word of warning.

Blodgett's wound severed a major artery below his right collarbone. Again yesterday, lawyers pressed their argument that he died not from the wound but from dubious medical practice at Sturdy Memorial Hospital, Attleboro.

But State Medical Examiner Joanne Richmond insisted the cause of death was "massive bleeding to a major blood vessel caused by the crossbow injury." When advised by Lutes that Dr. Elias Arous, a surgeon at UMASS where Blodgett died about 6½ hours after the shooting, described the cause of death a "cardiac arrest due to hemorrhaging shock," she suggested the meaning was basically the same.

In 1969 the Grahams lived in a two-bedroom apartment in Norwood, Massachusetts. Donald Graham owned a floor cleaning and shampooing business and was making decent money, but had no health insurance for himself or his family. His sons, Stephen and Stuart, were six and four. When number-three son Douglas was born, Don had to pay all expenses.

November 8, 1995 — *The Woonsocket Call,* **written by Russ Olivo, Staff Writer:**

Graham takes the stand

New Bedford, Mass. — Even as he testified in his defense, Donald S. Graham could not say for sure whether the Attleboro man he shot to death with a crossbow following a dispute on Interstate 95 last year lunged toward him with a flashlight during the fatal confrontation, a key element of his lawyers' self-defense theory.

Testifying in an often barely audible hush, the lanky 56-year-old Woonsocket church deacon admitted harassing motorist Michael Blodgett because he had seen him flash his high beams at another car, setting off a chase that ended in Blodgett's death.

But, under questioning by defense counsel David A. Cooper in Superior Court yesterday, Graham said that during the confrontation, moments before the shooting, he was unsure if Blodgett had lunged at him.

"I told them to hold it, stop right there," said Graham, referring also to Robert Astin, Blodgett's passenger. "He (Blodgett) erupted. He started screaming obscenities. I was backpedaling."

Armed with a Barnett Commando crossbow he pulled from his trunk as the men approached, Graham said he "presented the weapon" to them, clutching it against his midsection as a warning, still backing up.

"I warned them both again to stop," he said.

As Astin circled behind him, Blodgett approached closer, shining the flashlight in his face and blinding him, Graham said. Because of that, he said, he wasn't sure whether Blodgett had actually lunged toward him as his lawyers told jurors in their opening statement.

"At this point Mr. Blodgett is about arm's length away," said Graham. "He shone the lights in my eyes. I alerted him. As I did so, the crossbow discharged. I sensed commotion but I didn't see any."

Graham, who told jurors he raises "Himalayan cats" and dances in his spare time, said he had just gotten on the highway Feb. 20, 1994, after dance classes in Canton with his wife Sandra, a secretary at Woonsocket High School.

A few minutes later, he said, he saw Blodgett flash his high beams at another motorist, setting off what prosecutors have dubbed "the chase of death," which ended in the demise of the 42-year-old EMT for which Graham is facing a charge of first-degree murder.

"It sounds silly," said Graham. "I made a few mistakes in judgement here. I felt compassion for a driver who was being harassed for no more reason than telling someone to move over. I did that without considering the consequences or without examining how many people were in the car."

Graham said he began following Blodgett with his high beams on for about 30 minutes when the passenger in Blodgett's car threw a trash bag at him, leaned out the window "and gave me a one-finger salute." He said he should have taken it as a warning and considered breaking off the chase then, but didn't.

When Blodgett moved over from the high speed to the middle lane, Graham said he followed, but stayed further behind. Suddenly, Graham said he noticed Blodgett's car was slowing down and he was gaining on him.

Then, said Graham, Blodgett "slammed on his brakes," nearly causing him to rear-end Blodgett's car. While he was downshifting in "unbelievable" traffic, Blodgett rolled down his window and threw a drink at him.

"What was your state of mind at this time?" Cooper asked.

"Panic," he said. "I didn't know if we were going to be killed."

Graham said he turned off his high beams and tried to end the pursuit at that point, but Blodgett again slammed on his brakes. Then Blodgett pulled into the breakdown lane.

Graham testified he stopped behind Blodgett because he was afraid to pass him, saying, "either way I was going to get sideswiped." He pulled about 100 feet behind Blodgett's car and Blodgett and Astin immediately got out.

"I was going to wait them out while they cooled off. I knew they were furious about it," he said.

When he saw Blodgett approaching carrying something, Graham said he told his wife, "We have big trouble coming down on us." He said, "I don't know what type of weapon the driver had. I was scared. It was a time for tough choices. These guys were huge."

At one point, Graham asserted, "I didn't need a crystal ball to tell these men were dangerous. They were going to hurt me."

Under cross-examination by Asst. District Attorney John Letourneau, Graham readily conceded that he passed up at least two opportunities to end the chase.

"I continued because I felt if I passed him, he would run us off the road," said Graham.

Earlier, Sandra Graham testified she realized that her husband was following someone with his high beams on but didn't understand why. She asked her husband who said, "Did you see what that man did?"

After the trash bag came across the hood of their car and Blodgett braked, she said, "I was scared to death. I was so afraid there'd be a car behind us that wouldn't be able to stop."

During the confrontation in the breakdown lane, the two men walked "aggressively" toward their car, she said.

She opened the door but couldn't hear any conversation. She said she didn't see her husband fire the crossbow but they talked about contacting a lawyer and the police as they traveled directly to their Woonsocket home later.

Mrs. Graham, who has been sequestered during the trial, walked past her husband without looking at him after her testimony. The case could go to the jury today after final arguments.

The Grahams moved to Woonsocket, Rhode Island and settled into a two-family apartment house on Oakley Road in the north end of the city. The First Baptist Church of Woonsocket was the closest church to their home, less than a two-minute walk. Donald was a Baptist, so Sandy joined the church knowing he'd follow.

Took me twenty-nine minutes to get from an appointment in Woonsocket to my dentist's waiting room in North Providence. Now, when I drive, I look around. I go out of my way to be patient and courteous.

I arrived on time. Only to wait an hour. Ed Soforenko, an insurance colleague from Providence, was also in the waiting room. Ed's a tough-as-nails, old school, independent agent, who insures many of the state's jewelry manufacturers. He's the type who's forgotten more than most agents know.

"When the hell is good news gonna' come out of Woonsocket?" Ed asked with his usual caustic charm.

"You must have read about Donald Graham."

"Yes, I have."

"It's a hard story."

"Bad guy," Ed said.

"What do you mean, bad guy?" Every time I saw Ed Soforenko his nose was dripping and today was no exception.

"I don't like this Graham character." Ed ran his sleeve across his nose.

"That's certainly your prerogative, Ed. I find it hard to understand how quickly you can judge."

We went back and forth. I told him about my client/friendship relationship with Don and expressed my hopes for an acquittal. "Ed, I'm sure if you met Don, you'd like him."

"I wouldn't bet on that," Ed retorted. "To tell you the truth, the more I look into this case, the more I think you're backing the wrong horse. I consider him arrogant and I think he thinks he's above the law."

"I cannot agree with that."

"You don't have to. It's my guess Graham is going down."

I shook my head. "Hope you're wrong."

"I can see that, Dave. Bottom line, he's the one who shot the crossbow. He's the predator. He's the guy with the military experience. A marksman of his ability could have picked off five Blodgetts if he so desired."

"But he didn't, did he? Graham's an archer, not a hunter."

"Whatever. He's a crack marksman." Ed nodded, agreeing with himself. "I heard that Blodgett had a criminal record. Rape charges I believe. Ya know what I say to that? So what. Graham didn't know that out there on the highway. Fact is, Dave, you just can't shoot a man for turning on his bright lights. And I don't care what anyone says, if Graham wanted to get the hell out of there, he had ample opportunity. Hell, he could have had Blodgett follow him all the way to the Woonsocket Police Station. Bottom line, he killed a man. Can't do that. Hell, if he was in Texas, he'd get the chair."

"I don't think so, Ed. In Texas, they may have given him a medal."

The receptionist called Ed's name. He got up, gave me one of those distorted funky faces along with a shoulder shrug, wiped his nose, and headed for the desk.

Donald Graham changed occupations. He read in The Woonsocket Call *that General Motors was advertising for auto workers. He didn't even know GM had operations outside Detroit. He visited the plant in Framingham, Massachusetts and filled out an application. When they saw his military obligation was completed, they asked him to start that night. He began the second shift in the paint department. The work was so hard he had to run to keep up with the conveyor belt. It was the highest-paid factory work in Massachusetts; yet, they had to advertise in Rhode Island. Most new employees quit in less than a week.*

November 9, 1995 — Excerpts from *The Woonsocket Call* by Russ Olivo, Staff Writer:

Crossbow case goes to the jury

New Bedford, Mass. — Was Donald S. Graham warding off an attack when he shot a man with a crossbow on Interstate 95 last year, or was he punishing the motorist because he disapproved of his highway manner; ultimately ensnaring the victim in a deadly ambush?

That was the question put to the jurors yesterday as they began deliberations in the Superior Court murder trial of the seemingly mild-mannered, 56-year-old Woonsocket church deacon who is accused in the Feb. 20, 1994 slaying of Michael Blodgett, 42, an emergency medical technician from Attleboro.

Jurors deliberated for 3½ hours yesterday without reaching a verdict. The jury got the case following final summations from attorneys and instructions from Judge James McHugh, which open the door for a conviction on any one of four criminal charges, including first-degree murder. The crime carries a mandatory life sentence without parole.

Deliberations resume at 9 this morning.

Blodgett was shot below the right collarbone with an expanding razor-tip arrow after he and a passenger, Robert Astin, approached Graham in the breakdown lane in Mansfield, the culmination of a highway dispute over flashing high beams that Graham admittedly started.

Two vastly different interpretations of the evidence emerged as lawyers summarized four days of testimony yesterday before deliberations began.

"They were going to attack Mr. Graham," said defense counsel David A. Cooper. "Is he supposed to throw the crossbow down and let himself be beaten to death? Of course not. He had a God-given right to defend himself."

Cooper repeatedly accused the state's key witness, Astin, who testified that the shooting was unprovoked and Graham fired without a word of warning, of lying.

Despite having followed Blodgett for miles, said Cooper, his client was convinced that if he did anything to allow Blodgett's vehicle to get behind him that Blodgett might have run him off the road.

Witnesses testified the razor tip Graham used was manufactured precisely to cause death of big game by hemorrhaging, but Cooper argued "it wouldn't have made any difference" had Graham used a blunt target arrow because the shortage of blood at Sturdy Memorial Hospital would have still translated into death for Blodgett. "It's just like trying to put out a fire without a ladder," said Cooper.

But Asst. District Attorney John Letourneau said the "medical issue," as he put it, was a smokescreen, arguing the Sturdy doctors acted "heroically" to save a patient who was, in effect, dead on arrival.

"Blodgett died because of the arrow that was shot into him by this man," said Letourneau, pointing at Graham. "This medical issue is a non-issue. Even if it does exist, for the sake of argument, it does not excuse the criminal behavior of this man."

Invoking the very words of his opening "promise" to the jury, Letourneau said Graham was a man who set it upon himself to "be a guardian of the highway to avenge" behavior he disliked. He said Graham started the pursuit and opted to continue despite repeated opportunities to break it off before the confrontation came to a head.

Portraying Graham as archery-savvy, he said it was inconceivable the defendant had accidentally unlatched the trigger safety mechanism during the lengthy, deliberate series of motions required to fire the weapon — actions he said supported the theory of first-degree, or premeditated murder. He also told jurors they could justify the same charge merely because of the nature of the bolt used.

After being chased for miles, Blodgett "deserved an explanation," he said. But Graham "never said a word," shielding himself behind the trunk while lying in wait as Blodgett approached him.

"In fact I suggest to you what we have here was an ambush," said Letourneau. "He kept the trunk lid open until he could get a bead on his victim. He never said a word and he shot Mr. Blodgett to death."

Beyond first-degree murder, McHugh said jurors could find Graham guilty of second-degree murder, voluntary manslaughter or involuntary manslaughter, or acquit him. In order to find him guilty of first-degree murder, there must exist evidence of premeditation or one of seven aggravating conditions, including the defendant's "indifference" or the nature of the weapon.

Every assignment Graham ever had at General Motors he figured out a way to make it easier. And every time he made it easier, GM figured out a way to eliminate the job. But, he persevered up to the day they closed their Framingham plant in 1989. Graham already had twenty years of service and was working part-time as a bookkeeper for a nonprofit organization. He opted for retirement.

The first fifty years of Donald Graham's life were productive and rewarding. Growing up in New Brunswick; having two sets of parents; a successful high school career culminating in achievements as class president and valedictorian; and traveling in Canada with his father. Moving to the United States; meeting and marrying Sandra. A member of the famed 101st Airborne Division. Three kids. All those years at General Motors. It was time to retire and have some fun.

Thursday, November 10, 1995

Today, after ten hours of deliberation over two days, the six male, six female jury came to a decision. Guilty of First Degree Murder with a Sentence of Life Imprisonment Without a Chance for Parole.

Upon hearing the decree Sandra Graham sat expressionless. Agnes Smith's agonizing moans could be heard from New Bedford, Massachusetts all the way to Fredericton, New Brunswick.

In today's *Woonsocket Call,* Russ Olivo wrote:

As he sentenced Graham, McHugh said: "This clearly was an incident of enormously tragic proportions... To some people this may be viewed as a paradigm of life on the highway. To me it is simply a matter of individual responsibility that must be individually taken."

Donald stood poker-faced and in shock while facing the jury. The Judge asked him if he had anything to say, and he replied, "Nothing Your Honor." It was four in the afternoon and the prisoner, shackled hands on a waist chain, was led by marshals into a Bristol County Sheriff's van.

Mad.

That was my first reaction. Mad at Donald for doing what he did. Madder at Donald's counsel for losing the case. And maddest at the jury. How could six men and six women arrive at *life without parole?* Heinous, hard-nosed, repeat offenders get life without parole. Donald Graham fits none of those roles. Granted, as the case unfolded, and Asst. D.A. Letourneau squeezed the vise, I questioned Don's judgment. Hell, in testimony, Donald questioned his own judgment. But, *life without parole?*

I have so many questions I don't know where to begin:

Why did the jury believe Astin and not Graham?

What did the jury think Blodgett and Astin were going to do as they stalked toward Graham, pin a gold medal on Don's shoulder?

Why didn't the defense counsel go with temporary insanity?

How could they not get a sentence of manslaughter?

I wish I had been at the trial. As it unfolded there was endless scuttlebutt exchanged in Woonsocket.

Blodgett had multiple criminal records including rape. Why no media coverage on that issue?

The car Blodgett was originally high-beaming was occupied by a young female. Why wasn't this played to the hilt by the defense?

Donald could have made a better witness, and softened his demeanor; but, he didn't. He stayed bitter and hard. No remorse crossed his countenance. Bottom line, he believes what he did was right. He protected Sandra and himself, an act of self-defense.

When the jury deliberated into a second day, first-degree loomed as a more probable outcome. The Graham crowd sensed a Rhode Islander was being railroaded in Massachusetts.

Think about it, one minute they're round dancing and now life without parole. Poor Sandra, the kids, the church, Woonsocket. Don, why didn't you just keep driving?

November 13, 1995 — *The Woonsocket Call,* **written by Russ Olivo, Staff Reporter:**

Graham's attorneys file for a new trial

Woonsocket — Lawyers for crossbow killer Donald S. Graham will file a motion for a new trial today, arguing their client was portrayed as "some kind of nut" because jurors were allowed to view four crossbows seized from his home in addition to the murder weapon.

Lawyer Scott Lutes said he and cocounsel David A. Cooper objected to jurors seeing the other crossbows on grounds they were irrelevant to the slaying of Michael Blodgett. But they were overruled by Judge James McHugh.

And that's it? Seems to me Don's lawyers couldn't get away from his case fast enough. If all they're contending is the crossbow issue, I think they're coming up pitifully short.

Chapter Four

Road Rage and Big Time TV

My longtime friend, Bob Golden, called to discuss the incident. He suggested I search online for the origin of the term "road rage," which I did. This is what Wikipedia explains:

"The term originated in the United States during the 1980s, specifically from Newscasters at KTLA, a local television station in Los Angeles. In 1987–1988, a rash of freeway shootings occurred on the 405, 110 and 10 freeways in Los Angeles..."

There are other sources that attribute the origin to rash and unruly roadside events in England. Regardless, road rage came to life for me on that dreadful February night in 1994.

In August 1997, almost two years after the verdict, I received a telephone call from Gil Perez. He was very animated. "David, I have good news about Donald Graham. CBS is coming to Woonsocket to do a story on their *48 Hours* program."

Gil, a member of the First Baptist Church of Woonsocket, like Don, is also a deacon, who works full-time for Woonsocket Family Resources. Gil and I always laughed when I accused him of being the only Baptist in Woonsocket with a Puerto Rican accent.

"The subject is going to be about road rage in America," Gil advised. "From what I understand, Dan Rather has already interviewed Donald and he's coming to Woonsocket to interview us."

"How do you know all this, Gil?

"Paul LaRosa called the church. He's the producer of the show."

"Very interesting. That's quite a combination — CBS, Dan Rather, and Woonsocket. With road rage being the focus I don't think this is going to be a very happy show."

"But maybe it'll shed some positive light on Donald."

"Maybe it will, Gil. I sure hope so."

But, my first reaction was not as positive as Gil's. Not too sure why. Perhaps it was my prevailing negative mood. For the past few years I'd been in a grand funk from a handful of serious problems. Besides the Donald Graham tragedy, both my parents had recently died. My only brother and I were not on speaking terms due to a business rift. And I had recently divorced. Not good.

Woonsocket was doing no better. A series of sour events enshrouded the city. Another murder case unfolded, which involved "Beaver" Tempest, the son of Ray Tempest, a popular, former head of the detective division for the Woonsocket Police Department. Ray later became the High Sheriff of Providence Plantations. And Woonsocket was center stage in the Rhode Island banking crisis of the early 90s. Marquette Credit Union, the state's largest credit union, located in Woonsocket, was being charged with mishandling its money. When Rhode Island Governor Bruce Sundlun closed the bank down and personal savings accounts were frozen, Woonsocket became a disaster area.

The only positive Woonsocket news came from the top of Logee Street, which domiciles the Mount Saint Charles Academy hockey team. The "Mounties" had won 17 consecutive high school state championships and during eight of those years they were national champs.

"Hey David, would you come to the church and be one of the interviewees?" Gil asked.

"Me?"

"Yes. We need you, David. We know you will represent the sentiments of the parish. That you'll tell them right. Will you come?"

"Of course I'll come."

I went. With all my heart and soul, bound by a conviction that Don's verdict was wrong and I could make a difference. Paul LaRosa, CBS producer of *48 Hours*, conducted the interview. It lasted about five minutes. I was emphatic in my comments that Don got a raw deal.

The program appeared on the evening of September 11, 1997. Fired up, my emotions were dual-edged. The anticipation of appearing on national TV was exciting, my 15 seconds of fame so to speak. And, most importantly, this could benefit Don. An opportunity for millions of Americans to hear his side of the story. I hoped the far reaching voice of *48 Hours* would influence the powers to be; the case would be reopened, and his sentence changed. Yes, that's what I was hoping, even praying for, along with Don's family, friends, and all the members of his church.

I leaned into my television totally absorbed. Dan Rather set the record that the subject matter was road rage, a developing problem all across the country.

The camera panned several cameos of road rage incidents. Then the focus became Donald S. Graham.

Rather's interview of Don was spine-chilling. By then, he had been stewing behind bars for close to two years. His face was pallid behind thick glasses that showed riveting eyes. His body language said, "I'm innocent and have been screwed by the system." And that's pretty much what he said, with bitterness and contempt.

Near the end of the program, Rather commented, "You know what I haven't heard, it occurs to me, I haven't heard you say, 'I'm sorry.'"

Don responded, "You haven't heard me say I'm sorry. Well, I'm sorry that it happened. I wish it hadn't happened."

"You're sorry that it happened," Rather said, "but you're not sorry that you did it?"

Don said, "I'm sorry it happened. I wish it hadn't happened. I'm sorry that I had to defend myself. I was forced to defend myself. And I will not apologize for defending my wife and defending my own life. I won't apologize for that. And I'm sorry for [blank], as simple as that, [blank]. I'm not going to apologize for doing the right thing. I did nothing wrong."

For anyone who did not know Don, his presentation and demeanor sent out terribly negative vibes. Almost Mansonesque. I could imagine viewers sitting by their TVs saying, "Hey, the guy may have gotten screwed, but who wants a wounded grizzly like that back on the streets?"

None of my interview was shown. I was seen, for a fleeting moment, sitting amongst parishioners at the church. Nor were any of the members' interviews shown.

Later that night I wondered why we were not heard. It's a qualified question. Our comments were of value and sent a definitive message that *"first-degree"* was a farce. Maybe someone of influence instructed *48 Hours* to squelch our comments? The plan was to paint Don as an ogre? Conjecture, yes, but the prosecution had spent time *ad nauseam* building Michael Blodgett as a good man, a model citizen. Conversely, they portrayed Don as a ruthless "guardian of the highway" and a calculating killer.

Dan Rather presented Don the same way Assistant District Attorney Letourneau did! He exemplified the definition of road rage. If this was a movie, Don might have won an Oscar as the archetypical road rager. While we all

hoped and prayed for help, the program accomplished its objective of display-
ing the sensational horrors of road rage. Don was simply a pawn, a perfect fall
guy for the show.

The air exhaled from my balloon. It was hard to see Don that way. Too
hard. It just seemed he was destined to remain in prison for the remainder of
his life. A feeling of let's-move-on manifested. My life was also filled with
hardships. Adding Don's onus compounded my negative energy. Hopeless-
ness set in. I remember rolling around in bed that night trying to fall asleep
with Johnny Cash's song, *Ira Hayes,* buzzing through my ears.

The evening of September 11, 1997 was not a fortuitous one for convict
Graham; 9/11, a bad date, one that lives in infamy!

I did write Don, once, while he was incarcerated at the MCI Cedar Junction prison in Walpole. He wrote back. His words were bitter, caustic, and filled
with anger, not unlike his countenance throughout the *48 Hours* program.

Threw the letter in the shit can. I had to break away.

Chapter Five

Ten Years Later

Sunday, April 24, 2005 — Santa Maria, California

I'm riding a horse. Strange, I am not a horseman. The closest I've come to horses was the paddock area at the old Lincoln Downs racetrack in Rhode Island.

The scenery looks like Joshua Tree National Park in the high desert of California. My horse is walking along the top of a mesa, when suddenly it rears up. We come to the edge.

I hear a noise and jump off the horse. I look over the edge. There's a small gnarly tree set in the side of the cliff. Someone is crying for help. Below, gripping a branch, is my friend, Don Graham. The cliff drops off at least a thousand feet into an abyss of rock and oblivion.

How can this be happening?

"David, where have you been?" Donald asks in desperation. His face is badly sunburnt looking like Clint Eastwood in *The Good, The Bad and the Ugly.* His hands are bloodied.

"I don't know."

"Well, I need you."

I can see the tree uprooting from the soil. The entire scene fades away like a reverse pan in a movie. Donald's words fade into the distance.

I'm beside myself.

Awakening in a frenzy I reach for the neck of my tee shirt, which is moist with sweat. I shiver in the cool bedroom air and glance at the clock. It's only midnight. Thank God, this was only a dream; a nightmare so vivid I could reach out and wipe away the dust and blood.

I walk downstairs and open the front door. A full moon hovers brightly in the southern skies over central California. Still half asleep, I realize it's three o'clock in the morning back in New England. I wonder if Don Graham is sleeping. Maybe he's having a nightmare about the desert.

Breathing in fresh air, I try to refocus my thoughts. I look up at the cratered moon, perfectly round and surrounded in haze, and give thanks for simply being free. My nightmare was so real. It exposed a miserable memory. Almost ten years have passed since Michael D. Blodgett's awful death at the hands of Donald S. Graham.

Since the incident I've had similar nightmares. Ones where I'm stalked by a predator. Another where I'm attacked by assailants — big, brawny bullies. I always awake before the punches fly. Then there's the recurring dream where I'm being scolded for an act I don't even know I've committed. A black-robed, Darth Vader-like judge slams his gavel and declares to a large audience that I'm guilty. What'd I do?

Then there's the conscious flashbacks. I've had visions of Don and Sandra Graham round dancing. I know how much they loved their dancing, but it makes me giggle. I just consider their favorite music to be hayseedy. As a beebop jazz lover, I can picture Dizzy Gillespie and Charley Parker laughing at their do-si-doing steps.

Shortly after the *48 Hours* fiasco, I retired from the insurance industry. I kept myself busy doing odd jobs. And in the last few years I've traveled cross country by car five times with Maureen, who's become a traveling nurse. This past January we drove from Rhode Island to Santa Maria, California, located on the central coast, just in time to watch the New England Patriots win the Super Bowl. When we left "Little Rhody" there were 30 inches of snow on the ground. We've had our share of rain this winter in California, but never snow, and rarely does the temperature get under 60 degrees.

In May we'll be driving all the way to Alaska to spend four months in the Last Frontier, fishing and sightseeing. A dream about to come true. But at the moment I cannot stop thinking about tonight's nightmare. It's been close to twelve years since I last saw Don and now I feel closer to him than ever before. In a way it haunts me to think of all the good times I've had, while he stagnates behind bars.

After his 1995 conviction and before the *48 Hours* program, I possessed an uncanny sense of guilt. I've always had a feeling I could have helped Don, even though I played no part in the entire affair. I attended none of the trial; knew nothing about his lawyers.

So why the guilt? Donald Graham has been a friend of mine for a long time. A good one with no *quid pro quo* requirements in our relationship. He was a good deacon. He adored his church. I visited his home. I admired Sandra, his family, even the Himalayan cats. Now, it vexes me that I've not stepped forward. There must be something I can do. Maybe I can prepare a series of articles and submit them to *The Woonsocket Call* or *The Providence Journal*, even *The Boston Globe.* A written plea to a top lawyer, or a request for pardon to Massachusetts Governor Mitt Romney. A book.

Outside Woonsocket and Attleboro, the Graham/Blodgett story is all but forgotten. Hell, it occurred in 1994. I had even forgotten several of the details. I need to restudy the facts, get updates. I need to call Rhode Island. I've forgotten the names of several players.

I shared my nightmare with Maureen and told her all about Donald Graham. She encouraged me to do whatever I felt necessary. I placed a call to Vic Blank in Cumberland, RI.

"You're bringing back an old canker sore, David. The reason I remember it so well is because of the verdict and sentence. First-degree and life without parole. It just didn't make sense."

"I want to do something about it."

"Like what?"

"Get him out of the slammer."

"That's very nice. When did you pass the bar exam?"

At times Vic acts out a complex, overly-witty game in conversation. He'll pretend simplemindedness and ask simpleminded questions, which in turn makes him look simple, in contrast to the brilliant mind he is. Maybe it's some form of unconscious guilt for being so smart, a reverse superiority complex, if there is such a thing. Enough to drive me crazy. But, I've been going along with it for years. I don't know. I just like Vic. Especially when I play him in gin rummy. "Not a good question, Vic. Do you remember Paul Dempster?"

"Vaguely. Who is he?"

"He passed away several years ago, but along with his wife and Donald they opened a soup kitchen in the basement of the First Baptist Church of Woonsocket. I forgot the name of the soup kitchen."

"Oh yes, we talked about that. But I can't remember either. Senior moments."

"Thanks, Vic."

"Hey, call Eddie Baram."

"Why Eddie?"

"Because he remembers everything."

"I thought you remembered everything."

"David, call him."

My first question to Eddie Baram was, "Do you remember a gal by the name of Pat Dempster?"

"She was married to Paul Dempster, who was a great guy. He was looked upon as a visionary. Paul went to the good folks at the First Baptist Church of Woonsocket on Blackstone Street to ask if he could open a ministry in the basement. Its purpose was to feed the poor; a soup kitchen."

"That helps, Ed."

"Good. Coincidentally, a few years ago, I volunteered for six months, serving soup and sandwiches. Dave, I'll tell ya somethin', I met a lot of characters there. I'll tell you something else unusual about that whole deal."

"What?"

"Paul Dempster's liaison with that church was the deacon, who was also the treasurer. You'll never guess who that guy was?"

"Donald Graham."

"Jeeze. Yes. Very good. Donald Graham, the infamous crossbow killer. Funny, but Mr. Graham had the same vision as Dempster to help the poor. Can you imagine."

"This I know."

"Funny, but talk around the soup kitchen was always favorable about Graham. Supposedly, he and Dempster became a team doing all they could to develop the kitchen. Ya know, Paul Dempster died several years ago. Terminal cancer."

"I know. I knew Paul. Used to visit with him at the Woonsocket Hospital, when he became sick. Seeing him on that hospital bed, a man of such energy, was sad, very sad."

"I bet." Eddie paused. "And now Paul's lovely wife, Pat Dempster, carries on the cause. Quite a cross to bear if I must say so myself."

"Well, I was trying to phone Mrs. Dempster, but could not find her through 411. Thought I might be able to contact her through the ministry, but I couldn't remember the ministry's name."

"You're getting old, David."

"We've already established that depressing fact and it doesn't make me happy, Eddie. What the hell is the name of that ministry? And does it still exist?"

"*Because He Lives.* And they're doing quite well, I might add. Want their telephone number?"

It had been eight years since I'd last spoken to Pat Dempster. As soon as I acknowledged myself over the phone, it was like talking to a long-lost companion. Told Pat that I sold my insurance business and was calling her from Santa Maria, California, the small agricultural town where the Michael Jackson trial was taking place. She got a kick out of the fact I returned to college and had taken several writing courses at Cuesta Community College in San Luis Obispo.

"Pat, now that I'm semiretired, I want to do something for Don Graham. As we speak, I don't even know if he's alive."

"Oh yes, David, Donald is with us alright. He's at the penitentiary in Shirley, Mass." Pat paused, her deep breath coming through the phone, "That's about all I know, I'm afraid. Both Sandra and he are in my daily prayers. Why don't you give Gil Perez or Pastor Roger Francis a call. They can fill you in better than I can."

She gave me their telephone numbers. "Actually Pat, I tried finding Gil and you in the telephone directory. Seems you're both unlisted."

"Yes we are, David. When I get home at night I'm exhausted and I know that's true for Gilbert. Otherwise, we'd never sleep."

"I understand. You helped, Pat. Thanks so much."

Before hanging up she said, "You cannot imagine how good Donald was to us throughout the years. Both he and Deacon Gil Perez. I don't think *Because He Lives* would have made it without their support."

"I know, I know. If you recall it was Don who introduced me to Paul. He wanted me to make sure the church's liability insurance provided coverage for the ministry."

"That's Deacon Donald Graham in a nutshell. And it was Donald who brought us all together."

"Strange, isn't it?"

"Sometimes we're only left with our faith. God's way, you know. Trials and tribulations. How I lost my husband. What happened to Donald. You probably don't know that Sandra Graham passed away."

"Oh no."

"Cancer, I'm afraid."

"I'm so sorry, Pat. That's not good at all."

"No it's not, David." We paused, reflectively, not knowing what to say. Pat broke the silence. "Look, you take good care of yourself and when you return home come and visit."

"Thanks, Pat. I'll call in advance. I love your pea soup."

She laughed. "I hope you can do something for Donald."

I hung up the phone. Paul Dempster and Sandra Graham both succumbed to cancer. It mortified me to think Don was in the slammer when Sandy died.

The last time I had spoken with Gil Perez was the day after the *48 Hours* program. Other than sounding older, Gil was the same energized guy. He told me he visited Don at both the Foxboro and Shirley penitentiaries, that this telephone call would inspire him to promptly revisit.

"Gil, can you give me Don's telephone number and his address?"

"Of course. You cannot call him, David. It's no social club." He laughed sardonically. "But please, go ahead and write him. I know it'll pick up his spirits. Why don't you come with me to the prison?"

"I'm in California, Gil."

"Oh my God. You're so far away."

"That doesn't mean I can't help. And I'm totally committed to doing that."

"That's wonderful to hear, David. Listen, you should contact Roger Francis."

"I remember Roger. He was the pastor of the church."

"Yes, that's right. Roger has visited with Donald and tried to reopen his case. He's done a lot and can help you out. Recently he moved to St. Petersburg in Florida. Hey David, when are you coming home?"

"Most likely in the fall, Gil."

"Well, we'll visit Don then."

"Damn right we will."

"David, I want you to call me if you need any help."

"Thanks Gil."

I reached Pastor Roger Francis the following day at his home in St. Pete. "Knew you'd be calling, David. Gil Perez gave me a heads-up."

There was a sense of urgency in his voice, as was true with my conversations with Pat Dempster and Gil Perez. Nervous energy. Felt like these calls were part of a *Mission Impossible* serial. Roger said, "I'll mail you several letters I've exchanged with Donald throughout the years. They're filled with information. It'll get you up to date."

"Thank you, Roger. How's Donald doing?"

"Last time I saw him he seemed OK."

"His spirits?"

"As well as could be expected. He's still a Red Sox fan." We both laughed out of astonishment and gratitude that the Sox were World Series Champs. "Donald's the same old finder, minder and grinder. Naturally this whole crime business has taken its toll. Sandra divorced him, you know, because he was sued in civil court by the other side and she had to protect her home. Very sad and hard to take. Then, she died a few years back."

"Pat Dempster told me."

"Oh yes, Don was allowed to attend the funeral," Roger said. "No sooner was it over, they shuffled him right back to prison. We all just stood there, silent, watching him step into the van with those awful metal shackles attached to his feet. So impersonal. Then, just like that, the vehicle was gone, and so was Donald."

"Sounds merciless."

"Heartbreaking." Roger sighed, "But, you know that Donald is a man of faith with a strong inner soul. A survivor. He wants to be free, David."

Hesitantly I replied, "Well, that's the mission here."

"Do you have a game plan?" Roger queried.

"I've got some ideas. First, I must review all the facts. There are so many twists and turns. Then I'll write. Actually Roger, I've already started writing and in time I'll complete a report. Then, I'm not sure; could submit to a newspaper or magazine. The right publication could present Don's story."

"No one has responded to the *Skowron Report*."

"*Skowron Report?* Any relation to the New York Yankee first baseman?"

"Right church, wrong pew, I think. Actually, John Skowron is a friend, part of Donald and Sandra's round dance group. Let's see, three years, yes, that's right. Three years ago John wrote a detailed report about Donald's case. Filled with valuable info. He even had it on a website. John took computer classes just to learn how to set up a website."

"That's what I call a good friend."

"Oh yes indeed. But, I'm afraid there have been no consequential responses to his report."

"I'd like to click on and take a look."

"That's no longer possible. It's shut down."

"Well, that's too bad. Are there copies available?"

"Yes. John would have them. Let me give you John's address and telephone number."

"Thanks. I appreciate that." I told Roger about my recent nightmare.

He replied, "The cause of conscience cannot be put to rest."

May 12, 2005

SBCC, P.O. Box 8000, Shirley, MA 01464-8000.

Dear Don:

So much to say, so much to tell, but, for the moment I want to abbreviate my words. Based on our lengthy friendship and my deep and sincere concern for your welfare, my mission is to do as much as possible to set you free.

For the last month I've been preparing a report which I'll entitle either, *Life Without Parole* or *Because He Lives.* As I write, I've broken my report into 8 sections and I could use your help. I've spoken with Pat Dempster, Gil Perez, and Pastor Roger Francis, who's sending me a copy of your last letter to him and other correspondence. Let's all team up to do as much as we can.

As I continue my report I'd like to know the following: Your DOB. Born where? How did you get to Woonsocket? What type of work did you do? Did you have any previous record? How did you get involved with the First Baptist Church of Woonsocket? Where is Attorney David Cooper? Who recommended him? What did he do wrong? How bad of a witness were you? In court did you say,

"I'd do it again?" I want any and all details of the incident. And, anything else you can tell me that will help overturn the verdict.

Roger indicated to me that you now have three months to plea bargain. I need to know all about that.

Some of my thoughts: I think there are forces from the "other side" that have protected Blodgett and Astin. You were railroaded by these forces to serve life w/o parole. I want my report to be an exposé, to raise the ire of the system(s) and the emotions of the public — to force reconsideration. To accomplish this it might take some creativity, like getting the report into the media or submitting a plea to Governor Romney — or any other suggestion.

It amazes me how time has passed. Gil told me about Sandra. My heart is with you.

Love and peace,

David Brown

PS: Here's a brief update of my doings: Sold insurance business in 1997. Now living in California. Will be off to Alaska on 5/26, and will return to RI in early Sept.

Roger Francis called back today.

"I've been thinking about your idea of preparing a report and sending the material to a newspaper. I question that wisdom. Remember David, the press was terribly injurious to Donald and they still may not look upon him favorably."

"That's a thought, Roger."

"Possibly I've become too much of a cynic. I just sense you must be careful who you deal with. So, take your time on that one."

"OK Roger. This is very difficult because I want positive results so quickly, yet it's going to take time preparing the report effectively."

"Yes, believe me, I understand. Another thing. Blodgett loved to play 'cops' and had a light on top of his vehicle that he could flash. Also, Don never hunted with the bow. He became an excellent shot and practiced only on targets."

He hesitated. "Did you know that Donald has a temper?"

"Can't say I do."

"Once, at a church meeting Don showed anger, but it was righteous anger, if there is such a thing, over an incident involving the church renting space to an irresponsible family. I suppose what I'm trying to say is Donald can get over-righteous on occasion."

Vic Blank wasted no time in mailing me the newspaper articles. He attached the following message:

> Dave, After a brief perusal of these reports, I have concluded that this guy is in a heap of trouble. You probably have more time to do some work on this than I. So, go to it — and feel free to call upon me to help write the legal briefs which hopefully, in time, will help to make a free man of DONALD GRAHAM. Vic."

Today, I also received the written material promised from Roger Francis, mostly letters exchanged between Don and him. Also included was a letter dated January 21, 2001 to Judge Nancy Gertner, United States Courthouse, 1 Courthouse Way, Boston, MA 02210. The letter is a lengthy, sensitive and personal one with a goal to influence the judge to reopen the case. I'm sure Roger spent a long time preparing it. What galls me, it's the spring of 2005, over four years later, and Judge Nancy Gertner never responded. Why? Roger H. Francis is a reverend emeritus. He deserves respect and courtesy. He deals with and cares for people as much as Gertner is supposed to, a judge representing the great Commonwealth of Massachusetts. And she can't drop him a line?

My mailbox contained a letter dispatched from the Souza-Baranowski Correctional Center. I walked it to my desk and carefully ran a thin knife across the top:

May 17, 2005

Dear David,

I received your letter and a note from Roger Francis yesterday. I appreciate your renewed interest in my case. Welcome aboard! I need all the help I can get. I never realized what sort of a Pandora's box I opened when I interfered with Michael Blodgett and Robert Astin that night. Just too bad it didn't happen seven or eight miles further south on I-95. Can you imagine the R.I. state police riding shot gun to protect a serial child rapist by creating a false scenario of me passing and cutting off Blodgett's vehicle several times in order to create "road rage" attributable to me? I do know that God has plans for everyone willing to listen to Him, and I suppose He has prompted you on my behalf.

The three months I have to plea bargain of which Roger spoke is the three months I have to appeal to the Supreme Court in Washington. They accept fewer than 1 case in 1,000. You can see the odds against me here. I prepared an introductory package to send to five different lawyers that I am interested in representing me. I sent the first one out over the weekend to Susan Stenger, who works out of Boston. I am enclosing a copy for your perusal as the package addresses many of the questions you raised.

To answer your questions: My previous record was related to motor vehicle violations of driving under the influence, and driving after suspension. My first apartment in Woonsocket was on Oakley Road, my landlord was Dr. Styborski, a local dentist, who lived in the other half of the duplex. He and his wife are deceased. First Baptist Church of Woonsocket was the closest church to our home, less than a two minute walk; I was a Baptist, so Sandy joined the church figuring (rightly) that I would follow. Brenton

Arthur was the pastor who baptized her. She had been raised in the Catholic faith (Weymouth, MA).

David Cooper has an office in Providence. A member of our congregation recommended Scott Lutes so Sandy hired Scott. Scott did not have a license to practice in Massachusetts but shared office space with David, who did. So Scott convinced me to bring David onboard as lead counsel. David was not prepared to present a "self-defense" defense in my case. He interviewed witnesses to Blodgett's prior bad acts and failed to bring them to testify to offset the prosecutor's evidence that Blodgett was an EMT who was interested in whether I needed help that night. He failed to produce medical testimony that would have shown the doctors never treated Blodgett's injury in his first hour and the nontreatment caused his death, when combined with the treatment he was actually given. And he failed to call any character witnesses among our friends in R.I. and Mass. In short, he gave a "bare-bones" defense.

Eight or nine years ago a prosecutor from Worcester told a gathering at a Christmas party that he "could convict a rock of first-degree murder; that's how easy it is in Massachusetts." I can't disagree with him.

Prior to trial I never knew that Cooper was a former Massachusetts prosecutor, and he instructed me to only answer the questions asked as briefly as possible. His only questions were directed as to what my actions were, and no questions to my feelings, emotions, etc. This way I was prevented from voicing my concerns and fear for our safety. I was not a good witness because he never asked the right questions for me to give an honest answer to.

Four crossbows that were larger and more powerful than the one I used to defend myself on the night of 2/20/94 were seized from my house and displayed at the foot of the judge's bench as I testified. Each one had a fearsome appearance and their cumulative effect was startlingly effective as the jurors passed by them, to and fro, as they went to the juror's box.

I could, and probably have, written a book on the incident.

Also, at issue, one that I never raised, is the misconduct of Judge McHugh. He now sits on the State Court of Appeals, a very powerful position. He is in violation of the Judicial Canon of Ethics, Canon 3 (A) (4), but I don't want to scare off any potential counsel until we have an agreement.

Are you familiar with, or aware of, the historical and categorical animus that Massachusetts has displayed against its neighbors, particularly Rhode Island? Until 1949 Massachusetts had a law that required its citizens "to shoot any known Rhode Islander in sight." It would still be on the books except for the intervention of then (RI) Governor John Pastore. I can recall highway signs threatening motorists entering the state with a 1-year jail sentence if they had a firearm in their vehicle. The first person executed in Harvard Yard was a Quaker woman accused of advocating peace with the local Indians in 1635.

I cannot help the fact that I am an alcoholic; perhaps 10% of humanity is similarly afflicted. Despite the recognition of alcoholism as a diagnosable and treatable malady, it is evident that alcoholics will always be pariahs. And public attitudes are unlikely to change. After the Mass. Registry revoked my license to operate, they phoned my wife's insurance company and told them that I was still driving a vehicle registered to her. This was an absolute lie, and it caused Metropolitan to cancel her insurance. This cancellation caused her new rates to skyrocket. This is how state agencies work to undermine the families of those charged with a crime. The Registry also lied to a reporter for the Providence Journal, telling him my DUIs were in the '80s and '90s. This had the effect of prejudicing the jury pool against me.

The forces against me include the media. The media depends on prosecutors/police for their livelihood, and I was just fuel for their business. They will not bite the hand that feeds them. Perhaps you will have more luck than I have had; journalists have a jaded eye towards those whom they have helped to convict. Maybe when 10% of the population is under lock and key they may be enlightened to their role in the American judicial system where a man, today, is required to prove himself innocent.

I agree with you about how fast time has flown. Come September, Sandra will be gone six years. Bill Wilson and Bob Smith, the cofounders of Alcoholics Anonymous, made the observation that alcoholics seem to be borne with the gift of attracting and marrying the world's finest women. Although I don't know why this is so, I agree with them. Unfortunately, the world's finest women don't always live to ripe old ages. Brain tumors don't discriminate. As it says in Ecclesiastes, "I saw under the sun that the race is not to the swift nor the battle to the strong, neither yet bread to the wise, nor yet richer to men of understanding, nor yet favor to men of skill, but time and chance happenth to them all." Not that I get any great comfort from those words, nor the verse that precedes and follows. But this verse explains life.

I saw John Lennon singing a song of praise when his son Julien was born — part of the song had these words, "Life is what happens when you are busy making other plans."

And how prophetic! The story of life is much the story of the unexpected things that happen to us along that road. The unexpected will always confront us. Your offer of assistance is unexpected, but I certainly welcome it. I wish you better luck than I've had so far. Looking forward to seeing you in September.

Sincerely,

Don

These are not the words of your average ruthless killer. Bitter — yes. Ruthless — definitely not. Never expected such a long letter. I was pleased. Smiled to myself, remembering Don's dry sense of humor. Only he could combine Alcoholics Anonymous, quotes from Ecclesiastes, and John Lennon in the same letter.

I contacted John Skowron, who was not as animated as Gil or Roger, certainly cordial and soft-spoken, but subdued. Skowron and Donald knew each other from the fun days of round dancing. He was brief with his words. His report, *Justice Denied ... The Cross Bow Murder Case,* was written in May 2002; however, he reedited in 2004 and asked if I'd like a copy of the revision. He also asked for my telephone number and address. "Feel free to contact me at any time." John Skowron talked like a courteous funeral director.

Things were happening fast. Everyone I've spoken to wants to lend a helping hand. Everyone questions the verdict. So, in short order I called the good Reverend Roger Francis, Gil Perez and Vic Blank, asking if they would join me as a member of "Team Graham." They all agreed.

Received another letter from Donald dated May 22, 2005:

Dear Dave,

I am enclosing a copy of the death certificate made out about 8 hours after Blodgett's death. The medical examiner listed a son, Edward, with an Attleboro address. The son is not listed as a survivor in his obituary in the Providence Journal. It struck me as very odd that a son with his surname was omitted, and two sons with different last names were listed. It seems to me that Edward requested that the funeral director not list him as a survivor for reasons known only to himself.

Michael Blodgett became a dangerous sexual predator in 1975; was allowed to plead guilty in return for a suspended sentence in 1977. And then was allowed to train and be certified as an EMT in 1978. Sometime after that he went to work for an ambulance company in Attleboro, Ager Trans Med, where his boss, William Fennessy fired him for actions he refused to specify to my investigator. Blodgett obviously had connections to have his criminal record sealed so he could be certified as an EMT in the Commonwealth. Ronald Blais, the lead Massachusetts trooper on the case, was a former Attleboro police officer, same age as Blodgett, and it is my guess, a classmate in high school days. Blais died from testicular cancer five years ago.

Michael Blodgett was a much more complex person than he appeared on the surface. Nineteen years after raping and sodomizing children he was out on the highway, cruising to entrap adult female motorists. How many years he did this can only be conjecture, but he wasn't completely unnoticed as his actions got him fired several years prior to my encounter with him. I think his son Edward knew what he was up to on 2/20/94. Michael was a very dangerous man because his EMT uniform provided perfect camouflage for a sexual predator. The uniform made it extremely difficult for the average person to spot the predator inside. Michael's life was a charade of the cruelest sort, an EMT by day and a predator at night, when he used a five cell police flashlight to blind his potential victims to avoid being identified.

And sexual predators are consummate risk takers. Twice, Mr. Blodgett stopped completely in the middle lane of I-95 South in 6 PM traffic, and to say he lived for the thrill of pursuit and conquest is an understatement. He was willing to get all four of us killed that night to satisfy his thirsts and to force me into the breakdown lane to avoid passing him.

Blodgett and Astin knew what they were doing when they marched down either side of my car, forcing me to retreat from it to avoid being attacked. By doing so, they effectively took my wife as a hostage. If they had succeeded in overcoming me and disarming me, what would they have done next? And then, what would they have done to Sandra? Would they have left a living witness, considering that their boss, Fennessey, had fired Blodgett several years earlier?

These are men who saw me racing to the trunk of my car, knowing I was not going after anything pleasant for them, and still, they opted to continue their pursuit of me, and seeing a dangerous weapon in my hands, still opted to attack me. For some strange reason predators find the chance of taking life-altering risks acceptable because of the thrills involved. I still find it somewhat incomprehensible that neither man was deterred by the weapon, especially since both saw me loading an arrow on it. I can only surmise that blinding his victims has worked in the past where a victim armed himself. He almost succeeded in disarming me; if the arrow had been several inches higher, or he had leaned back another inch, he would not have been harmed. Quite simply, he had bad luck that day. Predators don't get lucky all the time anyway; but, he shouldn't have died. His bad luck just never stopped until his heart gave out on him.

The Commonwealth was at fault for allowing a convicted child rapist to reinvent himself as an EMT. If you recall, he received a hero's funeral, as he and Astin supposedly came down to our car to see if we were okay.

Britain's most notorious serial killer was revealed a few years ago to be a "caring" physician who treated his victims in their homes. Ted Bundy was a slick-talking salesman. My point being that predators are good at concealing their true nature. And, of all strangers parents teach their children to trust, EMTs must be at the top of the list.

On or about 1993 the bodies of a dozen or more women were found by the sides of major highways in Bristol County, Massachustts. My wife, Sandy, and I were regular travelers on these roads in our square and round dance activities; so, as a precaution, I placed one of my crossbows in the trunk of my car. For whatever it's worth, after my tragic encounter on 2/20/94, there was no longer news of women found dead along these roads!

Regards,

Don

Dear Don:

Have received all your mail and documentations. To date, I've written 43 pages with intentions of consolidating it into a media package. Now I'm not sure. I'm feeling the only way I can present your case will take approximately 300 pages. A book. That's the way I want to go and I'd like your input.

Tomorrow we leave. I won't be writing as much while in Alaska (6/05 to 9/05). For me, fishing Alaska is a lifelong dream. Once I get home in September, I look forward to visiting with you and totally focusing on our project.

My best.

David

P.S. Logic dictates to me that because Michael Blodgett stopped first, he wasn't stopping out of compassion to help you. <u>You would have had to stop first</u> to make it physically possible to be helped. Just one of my many thoughts how this case was screwed up.

P.P.S. I sort of wish you had called me for a few legal references before you made your choice.

Late May 2005

Northward bound. Destination: Anchorage, Alaska.

While exiting Santa Maria, I drove north on Cook Street, right by the courthouse where Michael Jackson's trial is taking place. (Tom Misereau, Jackson's lead attorney, temporarily lived in our condo complex). The area was booming with business, catering to curiosity seekers, the out-of-town paparazzi, and press. The trial was in its waning stages.

I couldn't help but compare some of Misereau's strategies to that of Cooper and Lutes. Misereau's entire case was based on *character assassination,* whereas Graham's lawyers' attempt to bring to light Blodgett's criminal record of rapes, adulteries, and one charge of unnatural acts were disallowed by Judge McHugh.

To wit, Prosecutor John Letourneau took every opportunity through the media to assault Graham's character. One of his ploys was to portray Graham as a "highway guardian," and a dangerous driver who lost his driver's license due to alcoholism, which is true; but, Donald had been dry for close to twenty years at the time of the incident. Oh my.

The six-day drive to Anchorage made me feel like I was on assignment for National Geographic. Endless scenes of natural beauty. The day we exited the Yukon Territory and entered Alaska we saw bears, buffalos, sheep, and eagles. At each stop we met hospitable people. All my life I had wanted to visit Alaska. As an ardent fisherman, I salivated at the prospect of catching salmon and revelling in the beauty of our "Last Frontier."

On the other hand I had become obsessed with my Donald Graham mission. Nothing would get in my way other than a three-month sabbatical in Alaska.

I'll be having the time of my life, while Donald stews away in a penitentiary.

Sunday, June 13, 2005

Today's headline:

Michael Jackson acquitted.

ALASKAN TALE

As a youngster, I adored reading Jack London. Living in Rhode Island, his northwest adventures seemed so wonderfully remote. For me, London defined vicarious experience. I'd stay up late at night with my headlamp illuminating the pages and pine on his every word. Inside, I always possessed a fantasy that one day I'd pan for gold in the far reaches of the great northwestern country.

In August, I did. My landlord, Ron Gries, took me. On the drive out to Ron's secret panning site I thought he might blindfold me, so I could not reveal the location, nor how much gold we found. If I did, he'd have a contract out on me. Ron told me he was looking for a panning partner. I'm not sure if he was toying around with the idea that I might be a candidate. "There are two criteria to fill the bill," he said. "My man must be strong of back and weak of mind."

After hiking for a long time deep into the thick bush, he began telling me bear stories. One about his buddy and wife who flew down to their summer home in Soldotna. When the guy opened the front door he was greeted by a huge grizzly sow. He screamed and chased the bear right out of the house. He then grabbed his shot gun off the wall and dropped dead of a heart attack. Then, another pal took his dog out for a walk in the town of Tok and never returned. Neither did the dog.

Ron needs luckier friends.

We trekked deeper and deeper into the wilderness till we came upon a fast-moving brook. The water was icy cold, being fed by unseen mountains. Every so often Ron stopped and looked around. "Did you hear that?" I spent more time watching and waiting than I did panning. I believe it was all a ploy by Ron. He genuinely wanted this naive New Englander to get a taste, but never intended that I find gold. By midafternoon, when it started to rain hard, Ron asked if I wanted to stay the course. I gestured for us to leave, a sure sign that I was weak of mind. Strong bodies and weak minds; the type of men Don is constantly surrounded by.

* * *

There are so many stories I could share regarding our Alaska experience.

Suffice to say, I took copious notes and kept a detailed diary with hopes that in the future I'll write a book of short stories. It seems we were so occupied that sleep was eliminated from the equation. On several occasions we hiked along magnificent trails, saw moose and soaring bald eagles. We walked on glaciers, ate salmon, halibut, and Alaskan king crab. My oldest son Adam visited, as did Maureen's brothers and cousins. It's rewarding to host friends and relatives from the "Lower 48." Extra special because we're so far away from home and we can show off all the beauty. We maximized Alaska and loved every minute of it. As predicted, I did little writing.

* * *

We made a decision. We will not return to Rhode Island in September. Instead, Maureen has signed on for a three-month assignment at the University of San Francisco Medical Center. I realize this will delay my visits with Don in Massachusetts.

Arrived in San Francisco on Friday, September 16, 2005

We settled into a seventh-floor apartment on Locksley Avenue in the Parnassus district. Talk about culture shock.

I called Gail Johnson in Providence to discuss Donald Graham. Gail's a longtime friend who worked for the Providence Chamber of Commerce, and as a researcher for Ira Magaziner, who helped devise the healthcare package endorsed by the Clinton administration.

In the early 90s Gail was engaged to John O'Neil, one of Rhode Island's finest criminal lawyers. John introduced Gail to a young criminal attorney, Bob Mann. Shortly thereafter John tragically passed away from throat cancer. Gail once shared a comment made by John O'Neil. "No one spends as much time in the library as me … except Bob Mann."

Maybe Bob would be interested in helping out.

Gail suggested I contact the various news media. She did not agree with Roger Francis to be wary of the media. "Get it out. The press only thinks about now. They couldn't give a damn about the past. If it's hot, they'll go with it."

Vic Blank, on the other hand, recommends that we contact an attorney ASAP. Gail agreed with that. I expect that would cost big bucks. Knowing Donald has disdain for the judicial system as well as the media, this is all a catch-22.

Of the four people directly involved in this case, only two remain, Donald Graham and Robert Astin. They know all. And they have given different stories. Someone, or both, are lying. I've had a chance to get Donald's story. How do I get Astin's?

Maureen seems to think Astin would be receptive to talking. She thinks Blodgett and he were workmates, not necessarily friends. The newspaper articles seem to indicate otherwise. Maybe he'd be belligerent, even threatening. Or too scared to talk, scared off by the Blodgett clan, the police, the judicial system. Maybe, just maybe, he would be willing to open up. Even though he's a big guy, I imagine he was horrified when Blodgett got shot. And most likely upset that Blodgett had put him in a life-threatening position.

Dan Moreno, my favorite California fishing buddy, stopped by. He's become intrigued by the case and asked, "Can you talk to participants? Can you find one of Blodgett's rape victims?" Interesting question, It certainly would diminish Blodgett's character. However, during the trial Judge McHugh denied the defense the use of Blodgett's criminal record as testimony. Although it's a presumption the judge most likely would have denied the appearance and testimony of one of Blodgett's rape victims.

Dan then asked, "How about Robert Astin? Get to him. That would be a biggie."

Amazing we're all thinking about the same thing. Dan, Maureen, and I are focused on Astin. How to get to Astin is the $64 question. Maybe I could take a direct shot and call him. Tell him I'm writing a book and would like to conduct an interview. Maureen thinks it would work. Donald is certain he'd never talk.

So, Team Graham has two new members, Maureen Peterson and Dan Moreno.

Maureen O'Hanlon Peterson, my better half, has been there all along, from the moment I had the nightmare in Santa Maria, when Donald hung precariously from that high-desert branch. This also means she hears me talking to myself. Or acting out a court scene. I'm always the defense attorney. Plus, I catch her reading my daily work, which automatically qualifies her as a critic, which make's Mo devil's advocate *numero uno*. She's adept at creating the "third side" to every story. So many times she's said to me with dismay, "Why the hell didn't he just keep going?"

And I always chime in, "He didn't."

Then we go back and forth.

Maureen's being a traveling nurse has given us the freedom to seek out our most desirable destinations. A dream come true for many adventurers. We've driven cross country five times, logged residency in Seattle, and have covered the west coast from San Diego to Tatoosh Island, Washington. And now Alaska is a notch on our traveling belt. Each layover is about four months, so we rarely feel like tourists.

Major downside, we argue about getting a dog. The woman drives me nuts. I've had a dog. I adored my dog, a beautiful blue- and brown-eyed, long-haired Siberian husky. I miss dear Sasha. Would love to have another dog. But, we travel extensively. The thought of my dear Pathfinder smelling of doggy droppings eliminates any possibility. Yet, Maureen persists. She'll wake me at three in the morning and tell me about a dream she had about her dog.

Odd how our traveling odyssey began. After spending thirty years as an independent insurance agent, I sold my business in 1997. Thereafter, I became a multilevel-marketer for Excel Communications, which is a book in itself. And then in the spring of 2002, I retired. Just like that. And it has not been an easy transition. I still have insurance nightmares. Still get nervous on late Sunday afternoons. For a long time Mondays were weird because I wasn't at work. The upside is I can wake up late on Mondays and spend the entire morning reading the sports page. One such morning Maureen sat across from me over coffee and said, "I've never seen such a sad face. You look lost, like you don't know what you're going do for the rest of your life."

"You're right," I replied.

At the time Mo was nursing in the intensive care unit at Our Lady of Fatima hospital in North Providence. "Well, cheer up Neptune (she calls me that due to my penchant for fishing in the sea), I think I have a good idea."

"I could use a good idea."

"Remember when I told you about *traveling* nurses?"

We've been traveling ever since.

Like Maureen, Dan Moreno slipped into Team Graham via osmosis. Back in 2002, when Mo and I made our first cross-country trip, we lived in Castro Valley, a suburb of Oakland. Oftentimes, I'd drive Route 92 from Hayward, cross the San Mateo Bridge, and fish the ocean in Pacifica and Rockaway Beach. I found Danny on Linda Mar Beach in Pacifica one early morning combing the sand for a lure that he had managed to lose. We immediately became friends, especially when we found out that we're both handicapped with dyslexia. If Danny Boy and I were driving from San Fran to Los Angeles, we'd end up in Vegas, guaranteed. And go broke.

One day while talking on the phone, Dan asked me what I was writing about.

"A murder case."

"I thought you liked to write about funny stuff."

"I do."

"Murder ain't funny."

"Nor is my book."

Danny paused and said, "Moreno's my name and murder is my game."

I told him the entire story. I remember his reaction. "Let me get this straight, you're telling me a 55-year-old man, a deacon of his church, without any previous criminal convictions, got life without parole? You gotta be shittin' me."

Since that first conversation Dan has never stopped asking questions. He calls at any time of the day or night with the most curious of queries, then renders his opinion. Now, I feel Dan knows Donald as well as I do.

October 19, 2005

Yesterday, I received correspondence from the Reverend Roger Francis that contained a letter dated August 16, 1997 from Donald to Roger. Excerpts:

> Had my hair cut today and most of it stayed stuck to me, but the price was right. The barber did a half-decent job so I'll give him a bag of coffee to make him happy. There are some people that everyone has to be nice to and the prison barbers are up there at the top.
>
> I'm back at the "minimum" end of the prison again, after spending six (6) months in an isolation block for refusing a move to another prison where I didn't feel safe — a relative of Blodgett's is locked up there."

This letter was written just prior to the *48 Hours* program. Donald oozed confidence. He had great admiration for Dan Rather, who interviewed him for over two hours. Don told Rather to "just tell the truth." He felt the TV show would be helpful in overturning the verdict.

Also enclosed was a subsequent letter to Roger dated October 16, 1997, after the airing of *48 Hours*. Donald's words are solemnly laced with expressions of contempt toward Rather, who, in fact, did not show empathy for his side of the story. Donald noted that Prosecutor John Letourneau declined to be interviewed for the airing:

> Yet, he was Johnny-on-the-spot when the press was there to hear his lies; but he ran and hid when they came running for the truth.

Received a large envelope in the mail from John Skowron. He sent everything as promised, including what I've labeled the *Skowron Report.*

Along with his report Mr. Skowron mailed a list of prominent names related to the case. There are two new names: Christine Camara, who is listed as a reported stalking victim of Michael D. Blodgett, and Carl Sullivan, a man who allegedly had a highway encounter with Blodgett, similar to Graham's.

Letter from Don dated October 21, 2005:

Dear Dave,

You are correct in your observation that the average citizen has no interest in any of the "sorry asses" who are incarcerated. Most feel we belong here because we were convicted in the state courts and they think that justice is even-handed even though every defendant is made the object of a witch hunt. You can't have a trial in America without character assassination in the media by prosecutors who are all well trained in winning their cases in the court of public opinion prior to the trial. After this happens the judge will, of course, inform the jurors that the state must prove its case, as though that will overcome the bias that has been formed in the jury pool. Fat chance! This is why American prosecutors are so successful. Other democracies don't allow prosecutors to try their cases in the media.

"What is it like living in the can" is a very broad question. Living in prison is contrary to all of human nature and violates every human concept of life. Many men go crazy, and most in here are on some form of medication to control their emotions/moods/behavior. I have never had to use behavior-modification drugs, but that is not to say that I've not been afflicted by depression. I am just grateful that any of the low periods that have struck me have been of a short duration. I thank my faith for that.

My ten years of incarceration have all been in a Level 6 maximum security prison — 3 in Walpole and 7 here. In Walpole we were locked up 23 hours a day with one hour out of our cells for showers, telephone calls, etc. At SBCC the cellblocks have 2 tiers (34 cells on each tier) and a one-hour break period each morning, afternoon and evening, alternating 1st and 2nd breaks each day. To get a hot shower you must be out on 1st break in the morning or the water is lukewarm to cold the rest of the day. Each block has 8 telephones you can use at break. Three times a week we are allowed out into the yard (in lieu of tier time) and three times a week we are allowed to use the gym (rather than tier time). Three hours a week we can go to church or the library, or have tier time.

The cells are single occupant with a seat and writing desk (little over 4 sq. ft.) which is also used for a TV, if you have one. There is a 2 sq. ft. shelf for cosmetics over the bunk (30 inch bumpy mattress), This is the only air-conditioned prison in the state. The cells are made of prefab steel that were brought to the site and assembled. Cell doors are solid steel with a 4-by-18-inch window; they are computer controlled as are the lights.

All prisoners must stand for 3 daily counts at 6:30 a.m., 4:30 p.m., and 9:30 p.m. We can spend a maximum of $50 weekly in the prison canteen, which is noted for its overpriced merchandise. Boredom is the central core issue for prisoners and we all deal with that in our own ways. I have a TV and radio, which is important if just for exposure to the outside world. The only morning show I watch is Martha Stewart, mainly because she works hard for her guests to succeed and she never says bad things about people. Plus she has a wonderful voice and is attractive.

I attend Protestant services on Friday afternoon and Saturday nights, and Catholic services on Sunday mornings. Every second Monday night I attend the AA 12-step meeting; sometimes I chair the meeting when the outside AA group forgets to show up. My main activity during tier time is cribbage when we play partners. I'm the oldest man in the block and I team up with the next oldest, Bernard Sanderson, against any of the younger inmates.

I awake around 5:30 and begin my day with 40 minutes of prayer before the first "stand up"' at 6:30. Before breakfast I do my daily reading which includes AA readings from "Twelve Steps and Twelve Traditions." Then I have readings from three devotional guides: "Living Faith," "Upper Room" and "Our Daily Bread" with related Bible readings. Then I read a section from my favorite author, Loren Eisley's "The Unexpected Universe," an article from the current "AA Grapevine," and an article from Bill

Wilson's (AA founder), "The Language of the Heart." Then I conclude my morning readings with a selection from Robert Shafer's "From Bowulf to Thomas Hardy, Volume II," a book of English literature, mainly poetry. I also read a selection from the AA big book, "Alcoholics Anonymous." I mark each book where I finish each day so I know where to begin the next. I rely upon these to prepare me for the day (as well as my prayers).

My son Stephen sends me the Providence Journal; my uncle Dan sends me the Boston Globe and Christian Science Monitor; my aunt Agnes Smith sends me Canadian Geographic and John Skowron sends me Popular Mechanics. The rest of my reading material I pay from the $200 monthly sent me by Stephen.

I have access to other papers and magazines that are purchased by other inmates — I do all the crossword puzzles I can get my hands on — do my best to keep my mind as active as I can. Used to subscribe to Foreign Affairs and Readers Digest, but one is too pricey and the other too much advertising. More of my money goes to reading material than to canteen purchases. I am too heavy as it is and feeding my mind adds no weight.

Last month I was taken up to give urine on two occasions, four days apart. You have to pee in a bottle under close observation of a correction officer. A failure to do so means being lugged to the hole and fined over $100 to pay for costs of tests. I'm not in for a drug offense and I've never failed a urine test, yet they continue to harass me in this manner. Part of the price of shooting a protected pedophile.

Hope you have a sense of life at SBCC.

Yours,

Don

Going back to Don's very first letter to me dated May 17, 2005, he mentions Edwin and Agnes Smith, the aunt and uncle who raised him after Don's mom passed away in 1950. Included in the letter was their telephone number, so I called.

Agnes Smith answered the phone. When I told her my name and said I was calling from San Francisco, she responded with surety, "You're Donnie's friend! He's written to us all about you."

"He doesn't waste any time, does he, Mrs. Smith?"

"No he doesn't. Never did. Donnie's just like his mother when it comes to chores; you know, always committed to getting a job done." She gave a polite cough. "Say David, I'd be pleased if you called me Agnes instead of Mrs. Smith. It makes me feel younger, and I like that."

"Then Agnes it will be." I couldn't help but think of my mother, who always preferred to be called by her nickname, Dolly.

She continued, "Good, good. It's funny, but you sound the way Donnie described you and now I feel like I already know you."

"I like that, Agnes."

"So do I." She sighed. "I want to tell you a few things about our nephew, so you can better understand him. Inside stuff, you know, like Hollywood gossip. The truth is Donnie was quite the boy." She paused and I could hear her tell something to Ed. "Did you know Donnie was valedictorian of his high school class? Before then, he was more into sports, basketball, baseball and soccer; then, around his sophomore year of high school, he became more scholarly. He read everything from H.G. Wells to encyclopedias."

"I knew that he was a multifaceted person from my friendship with him in Woonsocket, so you don't surprise me."

"He worked and paid his way through college." She paused to collect her thoughts. "I'd like to believe that I had an influence on him. After all, David, I was an English teacher."

"I am certain you did, Agnes."

She talked about a few of Donald's friends, schoolmates, and his high school principal, Colin Barrett. "Donnie played bridge with Colin. That's not an easy game, eh? Personally, I didn't start playing until adulthood." She paused again. "You know, I've never told Mr. Barrett about what happened."

"No kidding." I thought for a second. "Agnes, maybe you should. Imagine if he found out some other way. Who knows, perhaps there's something helpful he can do."

"Oh my goodness, I never thought of that. Maybe I should give him a call."

"Think about it, Agnes."

"I think I'll take your advice."

"Good. Ya know, I'm really happy I made this call. I consider our conversation very special, and I want you to feel free to contact me at any time, OK?"

"Thank you so much, David. Before you hang up, I want you to know how thankful Ed and I are that you're trying for Donald."

"Oh, I do understand, Agnes."

"He is a good boy, David. And he should not be in jail. I can't begin to tell you how many obstacles he overcame after his mother passed. Always working. Hitch-hiking to college on Mondays and back on Fridays. Paying for his education. Nothing came easy for him except his determination."

"We're both members of his fan club."

"We better stop or I'm going to cry." She hesitated, holding back emotions. "I'll tell you one last story." She paused again. "David, are you there?"

"Yes, I am."

"Thank goodness, you're so far away I thought I lost you."

"I'm with you, Agnes."

"Very good. Listen, I remember when Donald was thirteen. He wanted a bow and arrow. So bad. The boys next door had bows and arrows and targets, the whole shebang. That was the O'Ree family. Willie O'Ree became the first black to play in the National Hockey League. Donnie was always over there. Anyway, for Christmas Ed and I got him one. Wouldn't you know, he became so good at it, David, that we figured one day he'd win a medal in the Olympics."

"That's a story of irony, Agnes."

"I suppose it is. He'd never use that bow and arrow unless Ed or I were in the backyard with him."

Just got off the phone with Dan Moreno. Last week I gave him the *Skowron Report* to read and Dan was all upset because the report indicated that the transcript for the trial had been messed with. "If exposed, that could work in Graham's favor, right?"

"It would if I was judge."

"The presiding judge, His Excellency Judge James McHugh III, was obligated to pass along the transcript to the next highest court, so they could review the transcript to determine if there is merit for an appeal, a retrial."

"You're right. If McHugh's involved, it's like playing against a stacked deck."

"That's a freaking understatement. McHugh sat on that transcript for over two years."

"Not good."

"So, according to this *Skowron Report,* the upper court finally gets this revised, ragamuffin transcript and they turn our boy down?"

"You're doing your homework, Daniel."

"Thanks. That just ain't right. How can this be exposed?"

Over the phone Vic Blank announced, "Tell ya right now, our New England Patriots are in dire straights this coming Sunday. Their entire defensive backfield is on the fritz, not to mention a few of our defensive linemen are down, as well as our running backs. Peyton Manning should be able to pick us apart."

"Stay away from them, Vic. I know you love our Patsies, but don't even go telling me you took the points."

"I'm not that crazy."

"Good. What else is new, Vic?"

Vic completed his reading of the *Skowron Report* and talked with his lawyer. Immediately, the lawyer recognized the case and said Graham would *never* get a retrial.

"What?"

"That's what he said."

"What the hell does this guy know. You're pissing me off, Vic."

"Did you know that in the Commonwealth of Massachusetts, a first-degree conviction *automatically* warrants life without parole."

"Yes, I know that."

"Did you know that the Supreme Court of Massachusetts denied Don Graham an appeal *already?*"

"Did you know that Judge James McHugh sits on the Massachusetts Board of Appeals?" I replied. "The very judge who sentenced Donald. Did you know that?"

"Sure doesn't stand Graham in good stead."

"No shit."

Long pause. I could feel Vic thinking. Two laymen trying to maneuver across a lawyer's playing field. "That doesn't mean we throw in the towel," I said.

Vic paused before responding. "He's not going to get a retrial."

I paused. "I'm not going to accept that."

"Don't. There's another avenue."

"Governor's reprieve?"

"Good response. Yes, a pardon from Massachusetts Governor Mitt Romney."

"I still believe Donald can be retried."

"I believe that time is of the essence. None of us are getting any younger. Somehow, something has to be done ASAP. I'd love to get a guy like Alan Dershowitz involved. This is the kind of creative attorney that could lend additional light…"

"Thought you just said there's no chance for a retrial?"

"I did?"

"Now I like the way you're talking, Vic."

"Hey, your book might not be published for three years. If there's a way we can help to speed the process…"

"Let's go for it."

"Precisely."

"Now I'm feeling much better. Have you written to Don?"

"We're thinking along the same lines. I'm about to do that."

"I know he'd be pleased to hear from you."

"Good. Now I'm feeling better too."

"Hey, Vic."

"What?"

"Don't go bettin' on the Patriots."

"Let's get a lawyer."

Tuesday, November 11, 2005

The New England Patriots got glommed by the Indianapolis Colts on Monday Night Football in front of the whole country.

Danny Moreno and I went fishing today on a glorious, warm and sunny Bay Area morning. Great day to be above the grass.

Heading north from Pacifica, across the Golden Gate Bridge, we were fired up with hopes of hooking a few striped bass. I was fired up simply by being an east-coaster cruising the west coast along cliffs and switchbacks, with the blue Pacific Ocean below and the lighter blue Pacific sky above. Alcatraz clearly seen in the distance. As well as the great city, San Francisco, overloaded with a population of international consequence. The modern, towering, downtown skyscrapers. The buzz and perpetual movement. Twin Peaks and the Coit Tower appearing as stars atop a Christmas tree. Countless unique and pricey homes woven into so many districts.

Crossing the Richmond Bridge, we came upon a sign for San Quentin. The radio was blasting away as Janis Joplin coincidentally sang, *"Freedom's just another word for nothin' left to lose."* Danny said, *"Folsom Prison,* not *San Quentin,* that should be Donald Graham's fight song."

"What are you talking about?"

"Johnny Cash's song, *Folsom Prison.*" Danny smiled. "Do you know the words?"

"It's about the big boss ridin' on the train, smokin' his cigar, and movin' down the track?"

"Yeh, that's the deal. Johnny gets right to the root, *'I hear that whistle blowin'. I hang my head and cry.'* And he's dreaming about being free again. Just like we're hoping for Mr. Graham. So, it should be his fight song, our fight song."

"I think you got something there."

He turned down the radio. "Is Mr. Graham into music?"

"He is. Don's a big music fan; likes country."

"Country? That surprises me."

"Hey, he dances to it. It's called round dancing. Not exactly my cup of tea. It's a far cry from *Round Midnight* and Dizzy and Yard, but who cares, the guy loves his music."

"I'm an ole Cal-I-fornia boy. We all got a little shit kicker in us."

"No doubt. Johnny Cash is cash, a Hall of Famer. How bout *Man in Black* and *The Circle Won't Be Broken.*"

"The actual title of that song is *Daddy Sang Bass.*"

"That's right. Where he sings, *'there's a silver lining behind every cloud...'*"

"That's the one."

"Yeh, I like that music. I get caught up listening to the lyrics. They're bluezy and hardcore. Makes me better understand Donald."

"Does he know about Bob Marley?"

"I don't know."

"*No Woman, No Cry* would tear him right up."

"No doubt. I'm sure *I Shot the Sheriff* would grab at his coat tails too. What do you think?"

"I think we should contact Bob Dylan and have him do a song about Mr. Donald Graham, just like he did with Hurricane Carter."

I'm driving Maureen to work. It's 06:30, dusky and grey, chilly and miserable, just like Mo's early-morning disposition. There's a tight drive-in circle on Parnassus that leads to the front door of the University of San Francisco's Medical Center. That's my destination, where I provide my sweetheart with front-door service.

Just as I'm taking my right into the circle, a cab cuts me off. Came from out of nowhere. I slammed on my brakes, nearly rear-ending this idiot. Mo's coffee goes flying. I'm incensed.

The cab pulls up to the front door. As his fare is getting out of the back seat, I pull in behind him. I can see the driver, a big guy, who's wearing a turban around his head. Maureen is running late and scoots for the door. I roll down my window. I spit out words that include "stupid, fucking, asshole, dumb, son-of-a-bitch, you coulda kilt us."

Then I got out of the car! And advanced.

The cab driver inched down his window and cursed me.

I continued to advance like a raging gladiator filled with venom and contempt. I'm about three paces from his door when he hits the accelerator and peels out, cursing me in a foreign tongue as he goes. You believe that?

Got back in my car. I see nurses and students whispering to each other, some with sympathetic faces, others with fear. I say to no one in particular, "That guy could have killed us." I take a few deep calming breaths; folks are dispersing, and I think, what the hell was I doing? What if he jumped out of his car? Suppose he had a gun?

In July 2002 Donald Graham submitted a writ of *habeas corpus* to the U.S. District Court for the District of Massachusetts. This 109-page document petitions for relief from Donald's alleged "unconstitutional confinement." The writ objects to several events that occurred during the trial, all implicitly written about in John Skowron's report.

One objection that caught my eye pertains to a private investigator's findings. He was hired by Donald's attorneys. The investigator produced Michael Blodgett's police record exposing Blodgett as a rapist, philanderer and performer of "unnatural acts." This information was declared as inadmissible in court by the presiding judge, James McHugh.

Graham's writ reads, "Counsel's failure at this point in the trial to be familiar with Federal case law that permits (actually *requires)* this evidence *to be* produced at trial…"

What does this mean? To my understanding it means that at some point *after* Don's trial, the Federal Court made admissible these criminal-type records. So, if the new guidelines allow a judge to *include* these records, and the judge, *on appeal,* disallows the inclusion of these records and the defending attorney doesn't call for a retrial, something is wrong here.

I'm thinking about Michael Jackson roaming free as a result of his attorney arguing character assassination.

I received a letter from Mr. Colin Barrett, Donald's high school principal. Its paper was crisp. The Canadian stamp had a face on it, Saint John. It was neatly typed except for Colin's signature, which validated his age of over 90. The words from this letter flowed onto the page, "Donald was an eager and affable honor student. Friendly, happy, and talkative; his congenial disposition found favour with both fellow students and teachers."

Mr. Barrett enclosed a few photos of "Donnie," as well as his valedictorian address.

The Grahams —
sister Darlene, parents Elva and Frank, and Donald (circa 1950)

Maureen and I are having difficulty deciding where to go after this assignment at the University of San Francisco. It ends in two weeks.

So Mo hit the computer and ran a few inquiries. Really, what was holding us back was our craving for Alaska. We figured spending a winter there would be brutal. Our original traveling plans had made one thing perfectly clear, to never spend another winter in the cold. On the flip, pay for traveling nurses during the winter is very rewarding in a cold outpost like Alaska. Tough decision. We already had an informal game plan of returning to Alaska in the spring and to start looking for a condo.

But Alaska is so special. Sacrifice would be OK. Hell, it would act as a discipline for me to structure a rigid schedule of rest, good diet, and exercise. We could go Northern Lights *(aurora borealis)* chasing, cash in on a few hockey games, along with the Iditarod Race. And most importantly, I'll spend countless hours writing.

So we made a decision. We'll return to Anchorage. Already made arrangements to live in a downtown apartment on Cordova Street. Pathfinder and I will leave early Wednesday morning, December 7, 2005, and drive from San Francisco to Bellingham, Washington. Then I'll board a ferry and travel over 2,500 miles.

For the second time in less than a year I'll be postponing my Donald Graham project because of Alaska. During last year's stay I constantly fished. This time around, I'll write for days on end from mid-December to early May with a goal of finishing the first draft. In the merry month of May, I'll take a writing respite, remove my rods and reels from hibernation, and hit the fishin' trail. This is what they call a win/win situation. To set Donald free would make it a three-bagger.

Chapter Six

Back to the Last Frontier

December 10, 2005 on board the M/V Victoria

The enormous and ubiquitous wilderness is what fascinated me the most about my six day ferry ride experience. Except for a few ports like Ketchikan, Juneau and Yakutat, I saw nary a road, streetlight or building. Just wilderness, or "bush" as it's called by Alaskans. Never have I felt such a profound sense of freedom. The M/V Victoria is a ship of great proportions, over a football field long. She has been steadily sailing north through the Inside Passage at a speed of 17 knots. Now, it's late at night and I'm standing on the fantail, which protects me from the wind, and scanning the sky in search of the elusive *aurora borealis.* No luck tonight; too much cloud cover.

My thoughts turn to Donald and then to a book I read long ago, *In Search of the Miraculous* by P.D. Ouspensky. I remembered that P.D. stands for Peter Demianovich. He was no devilish man, but a brilliant physicist, mathematician and psychologist, a traveler and humanitarian. The kind of mind that could conjure up miracles.

The major character in *Miraculous* is Gurdjieff, whom the narrator refers to as G. The book is loaded with theories. Gurdjieff claims our globe is enclosed in a shell and we're controlled by a greater form of intelligence, as though we are puppets on a string. This concept has an uncanny similarity to the workings of the *aurora borealis,* where explosions blast off the sun and travel only so close to the earth, about eighty miles. They bounce off an invisible shell surrounding the earth and splatter, forming incredible light patterns around the impenetrable shell. The sun is the core; the lights are the puppets. The shell is Donald's prison.

The Victoria made an overnight stop in Juneau. While exploring the area, my cell phone finally worked again near the Mendenhall Glacier. I wandered off to a protected nook and called Maureen to let her know where I was, very safe and slightly tipsy, and having a grand time. She told me to be careful and "Don't forget to pick me up at the Anchorage Airport on the 16th."

I then reached my son Luke in Chicago. "It's cold and windy," he said, "snow scheduled to fall anytime soon." He laughed at the notion that his father was so far away, while he was boarding a bus in "The Loop."

I spoke to Danny Moreno in California, who was unloading a tractor-trailer in Oakland. It was 65 degrees in the shade. "I'm staying in Oakland and meeting up with Kenny Jones and Dave Martinez tonight. We're going to Yoshi's (my all-time favorite jazz venue) to see Maseo Parker."

My last call was to Vic Blank, back in Rhode Island. Amazing how clear his voice sounded. We talked about New England Patriot football. He told me that Syvia Medoff had died, a longtime neighbor and friend of my parents. Flashes of her husband Ed appeared in my memory bank. Ed was a doctor. Ed's brother Sam was a mill owner and entrepreneur. I took their daughter, Joanne, to my high school freshman frolic. All flashbacks of a former life in Woonsocket. We hung up. I was alone again. How odd I thought it was talking to those so close to me, yet so far away.

I felt serendipity surround me.
It struck strong like the crest of a wave.
I scanned the Mendenhall wilderness.
The greatness of the glacier pure white to glistening blue.
The vastness of the big sky.
Silence.

A black raven winged high from a dead spruce treetop and shrieked, a call of alarm living in the moment.

On board the M/V Kennecott in The Gulf of Alaska

I'm now on board the ferry, Kennecott, a smaller vessel than the Victoria, but more capable of handling open seas. If the bounce gets too rough, this state-of-the-art ship has wings that open from the hull. But we sail on a calm Gulf of Alaska.

December 15, 2005

The Kennecott anchored in the Alaskan port of Whittier at 0600. It was a surprising forty-five degrees, balmy and rainy. In no time I'm off the ferry, through the Anton Anderson tunnel and onto Turnagain Arm. Everything is grey — the mountains, the water on the Arm, the sky. Made me feel grey.

Tomorrow night I'll pick up Maureen.

We've settled in at 1101 Cordova, Apartment 249, Anchorage, AK 99501.

My computer was sick for over a week, suffering from a Trojan virus. Imagine that. So, I carried her over to Best Buy, in the snow, deposited her with the Geek Squad. Forty-eight hours later and $160 poorer, my Trojan was removed.

I return to my project. I have a major concern; I have no ending to my book! This tale of woe may go on forever without resolve. I think that means we have to wait until either Donald dies or I die. Then, someone else can be commissioned to write the final chapter. The perfect ending, of course, would be to announce Don's freedom.

Speaking of the unknown, I mean the unexpected, I met and talked to my new next-door neighbor, Ali Martinez. When I told him I'm writing a manuscript, he got very interested.

"What's it about?"

"It's nonfiction. About a man named Donald Graham."

"I've heard that name," Ali said.

"No you haven't. The setting is New England. We're in Alaska."

"Yes I have. What does he do?"

"Well, he's serving life without parole."

Ali's curiosity peaked. "In Massachusetts?"

"Yes, that's right. How'd you know that?"

"The crossbow killer."

"Holy shit."

"Amazing story. Happened in the early 90s as I recall. It got national coverage. I saw him on TV. All about road rage, right? Didn't the guy get screwed or something?"

Never in a million years did I expect that response. Never did I think Donald's notoriety would spread so far from home.

Gail Johnson called. "I just hung up with attorney Bob Mann. We had a lengthy conversation. He's in the stretch run of a trial, so he's <u>not</u> overwhelmed with cases. That's a good thing, timely. Bob will be glad to talk with Vic Blank about Mr. Graham's case. He started asking me for information, which I do not have."

"I'll call Vic right now."

A shot in the arm. Any kind of assistance Bob might give would be extremely helpful. I know Vic and Gail are pleased, because they've been banging away about getting a lawyer. I stood in the middle of the living room looking into a large mirror and shadow boxed.

January 13, 2006 — Friday the 13th and a Full Moon! (Hope it brings bad luck for the Denver Broncos.)

Agnes Smith just called from Moncton, New Brunswick. Eighty-seven years old and sharp as a nail. She wants to send me photographs.

Saturday, January 14, 2006

The Patriots lost to the Denver Broncos in the playoffs. Done for the season. With five turnovers, you'd think they were rooting for the Broncs. Oh my. Spring training is less than a month away and the Red Sox don't have a short-stop or center fielder.

Vic Blank reported that Gail Johnson had set up an appointment for him to meet with attorney Robert Mann on Friday afternoon. However, Vic did *not* meet with him. So, he took it upon himself to mail Mann the *Skowron Report*. This is what I call the "two strikes and you're out" routine. Leaving the ball in Bob Mann's court, knowing if he does not respond, we will not call him back. Worst-case scenario, Mann may never respond. Let's face it, he has the inalienable right not to. And we have no right in holding any malice. I'll sit on the edge of my seat waiting.

Actually, I can't even sit on the edge of the seat, because yesterday, while playing volleyball with the Anchorage Golden Buzzards (that's right, a group of old-timers who think they can jump like Bo Jangles), I severely damaged my heel. I've been on this health kick, an Alaskan New Year's resolution — eating right, walking, jogging, lifting weights. Then I found the "Golden Buzzards."

Yesterday, in only the first minute of the first game, I made a quick step back-wards, nothing dramatic, and pop, that's the sound my left ankle made. No one else heard the pop sound but me. I guess I felt the sound. At first I thought the man next to me stepped on the back of my sneaker. I even asked him. Then I looked down at my left ankle and it was dangling. Spent most of the day waiting in the emergency room at Elmendorf Air Force Base Hospital. Finally, I met with a doctor. I ruptured my Achilles tendon. The doctor suspects sur-gery will be necessary. When I finally returned home, Maureen was startled to see me on crutches.

Haven't had a good belly laugh in ages. Bottom line, spending so many long, dark and wintry days in Alaska has me off my game. Cabin fever, that's my latest malaise, which includes frustration. The fact that Vic Blank and Bob Mann did not meet is a perfect example. I can see Vic making the call. I can see Bob sitting at his messy, paper-strewn desk, being polite, yet knowing he's overloaded with other projects. Then I picture Don, sitting and waiting. And I sit here feeling like a dog trying to screw a football. Feel like I need a break in the action. Actually, I tried that and ended up in the hospital.

Understand, the inclusion of Bob Mann would be a major boost to our cause, but it did not happen, or it hasn't happened yet. Like every event in this frustrating, warped, fucking story, nothing ever seems to go right.

I need comedy.

From the scene of the incident, Astin drove Blodgett to the Sturdy Memorial Hospital in their hometown of Attleboro. The harrowing events that occurred there are unclear to me.

I have Donald's explanation, as well as John Skowron's report. Both paint alleged acts of malpractice on the part of the attending physician(s). Conjec-ture. Neither Don nor John were at the hospital.

I often wonder what Michael Blodgett and Robert Astin experienced on their way to Sturdy. Did they exchange words? Maybe Blodgett was more irate than anything else, belaboring the fact that this little bastard had the gall to shoot him. Could he feel blood draining, aware that his life was at stake?

Did he try to replay the scene and consider options that would have prevented this shooting? Did he realize this was no common arrowhead he ripped out of his shoulder, while standing near Donald's car? Did he think, at that moment, he made a mistake by pulling out the arrow and allowing blood to run freely? Or maybe he was mute, traumatized, and no longer lucid.

Certainly, every moment was precious.

Astin must've been beside himself as he drove south on 95, then Route 152 to the hospital. "This could be me" must have run through his mind. When they arrived, the scene had to be a madhouse. I envision an orderly or nurse taking a break, smoking a cigarette next to the emergency room door, and here comes two local EMTs. The car door opens, there's blood everywhere. Someone must have said, "That looks like one of our EMTs. My God, it's Mike Blodgett!"

Because Maureen is a nurse, she instinctively takes a defensive stance on behalf of the hospital staff. That influences me. The staff in this smalltown hospital had to be shocked to see a big bruiser soaking in blood and shot by an arrow.

Everything in those critical moments was consequential to Blodgett's survival and Donald Graham's conviction of murder in the first degree. Had Blodgett survived, Graham would not be in prison today. Seems to me, a research-intensive defense attorney would have a field day with the medical activities lasting nearly five hours at Sturdy. It was by far the longest segment of the entire incident before Michael David Blodgett was pronounced dead.

In the trial transcripts, Dr. Octavio Diaz, the first emergency room doctor who attended to Blodgett, was called as a witness. He claimed Blodgett had no pulse, that tension occurred on the pneumothorax. Which means either air or blood had built between the lung and pleura, a lung covering. This adversely affects the vessels to the heart. So he surgically opened the area and actually massaged the heart with his hand (Lord have mercy). Then he opened another hole on the right side. There is an alternative procedure; instead of all this surgery, he could have probed the area with a needle.

I wanted an outside opinion. I sent all the details to Dr. Martin Felder, former chief of surgery at the Miriam Hospital in Providence, Rhode Island.

There's a severe ying/yang to malpractice pursuit. On the one hand it could reveal that quality medical care would have saved Blodgett. If Blodgett lived, Graham couldn't be convicted of murder. On the other hand, testimony by the attending doctors could very well hold up. It did in the trial. The jury accepted that the Sturdy medical team gave their very best. I look forward to Dr. Felder's conclusions.

Another tidbit mentioned a few paragraphs back — if Blodgett hadn't pulled the arrow out, he might still be alive, because the arrow would have retarded bleeding. Most EMTs know that.

I spoke with Don's son, Stephen. He answered from his cell phone. He wasn't sure who I was. I brought him up to snuff. Soon, we got on the subject of the Dan Rather interview.

"My father thought Rather was his salvation. He never should have trusted that guy. He was looking for hot stuff and my father's cynicism was right up his alley."

"Maybe your dad wasn't the greatest witness, but his intentions..."

"Were good," Stephen interrupted. "Always good. My father speaks his piece..."

"To a fault," I interrupted.

"That's it, to a fault."

"Maybe you should give him some slack."

"I don't know. Maybe."

I reached down and stuffed two fingers into my fiberglass leg cast. I had a wicked itch. Just couldn't reach it. I explained that I was about 120 pages into the book, and my next step was to conduct interviews. Told him being in Alaska was an obvious proximity problem. I was hoping to find someone to help conduct those interviews. "Your father suggested I give you a call for help."

"He did?" Hesitation hung in the air.

"He also said you're a busy guy."

"He's right. I am busy. Working fifty hours a week, not including commute time. And we just had a baby eight days ago."

"Congratulations."

"Thanks, I'm on my way home now. Almost at a restaurant; I'm about to pick up an order to go."

"Stephen, I want you to know I've actually prepared questions for some of the interviews. I need someone to perform them."

"Look, I'm just driving up to the restaurant. I better pick up the food. I'd like to think about this. Can I call you tomorrow?"

"Sure."

"Good. Look, Mr. Brown, I want to help my father out. I'll help with the interviews."

"Good. We'll talk tomorrow."

"Tomorrow."

No sooner did I hang up, the phone rings. It's Vic Blank. I tell him about my conversation with Stephen. There's excitement in my voice.

Vic says, "Where has this kid been for the last ten years?"

"What?" I replied. A good question. I'd been having the same thought.

"There are three sons, right? I can't help but wonder why they aren't moving heaven on earth to free their father."

"I know. Hold your judgement, Vic. This is…"

"This is what? This is what I think; the kid's not going to call you back."

"I'll take that bet."

"Why?"

"Cuz I heard from the kid's soul."

"Right."

"Look Vic, there are reasons for everything. Some of them are beyond our comprehension. If Stephen doesn't call, it's OK. It's not for us to sit in judgement."

Below is an email I sent to Gail Johnson:

Dear Gail,

UPDATE: I spoke briefly with Bob Mann, Tuesday eve. Sounded very down to earth. Asked for my telephone number, he couldn't talk at the moment, but wants to discuss the matter. Not exactly my desired response, a sloppy-seconds feeling. At least I heard enthusiasm in his voice. So, I called back last night, forty-eight hours later, got a female colleague on the line, nice voice. She couldn't get over I was calling from Alaska. We exchanged temperatures. I gave her my cell phone number and email address. It sucks playing musical chairs.

If only I could fill Bob Mann with my emotions, I know he'd jump on board. Vic sure feels it. Actually, most anyone who gets to know Don feels it.

P.S. Yesterday, I spoke to Stephen Graham, Don's son. Interesting kid. Stephen WILL HELP in conducting interviews. I consider that a gold star. If Stephen conducts the interview, the interviewee will be less suspicious.

P.P.S. I managed to rupture my left Achilles tendon. Nothing serious, mind you. My foot and leg are encased in a fiberglass cast and crutches are needed. This will only be for six weeks, at which time I find out if surgery will be necessary. Other than that, everything is hunky dory.

My best,

David

Surprised that Stephen Graham did not call back. However, I did receive a letter from Don dated February 4, 2006:

Thanks for sending me a copy of my high school valedictorian speech. I might have added Hamlet's soliloquy, "To be or not to be — whether 'tis nobler in the minds of men to suffer the slings and arrows of outrageous fortune, or to take up arms against a sea of troubles." I guess there aren't second chances at such times.

Sandra was a very private person, somewhat of an introvert, and very shy. She graduated 16th in a high school class of over 500 in Weymouth, MA, which placed her in the top 4 percent of her class in 1960. As a worker she completed whatever she was doing, and did it well. She was faithful as a wife, an employee, and a member of our church. She was a great dance partner and organized all our dance weekends.

She was devastated by the charges brought against us. Initially, she was charged as an accessory to murder (another way to deflect attention away from the victim's criminal activities). My wife was quite pissed off at me and I can't blame her. She spent over a year meeting with a psychiatrist (once weekly). She became very withdrawn, and the first several weeks after Blodgett's death, refused to leave the house, even to go to work. The first time she left the house was to attend the funeral of Tom Dean, the husband of Dottie Dean, a round dance cuer in Rhode Island.

She didn't make a great witness, mainly because she was never asked any questions that would have made her a great witness. Cooper, our counsel ironically, and tragically, was careful not to expose Blodgett's character. Sandy committed herself to all that she undertook. In our square dance club, the Hill Top Promenaders, she was asked to be publicity chairman and she worked very hard to promote all our club's dances. The club president, Marcel Plante, said Sandra was the best the club ever had. The next club president, Will Roberts, told her the same thing. In church activities the women chose her president of the women's fellowship, she was a Sunday school teacher, served on the deaconate, was the church collector, and, until she died, was the church moderator. The moderator is the highest secular position in a Baptist church.

Much of the goodwill the community had for me resulted from the fact that I was her husband. I should mention that her life was affected by the fact that she was married to an alcoholic. Our marriage survived my alcoholism probably because I never cheated on her. Our marriage didn't survive my conviction, among other things, she was being sued by Blodgett's family, and so needed to separate herself, legally, from me. I still consider it a privilege that God allowed me to be her husband. To the best of my knowledge, I was the only man she ever knew.

If I'd left Blodgett alone all my problems would have been avoided. And she might still be alive.

Regards, Don

"I would have shot first and asked questions later." I could feel Vic Blank pointing his finger.

"No you wouldn't," I replied. "You wouldn't have the balls to shoot."

"I wouldn't, huh?" We were 5,000 miles apart. Yet it sounded like we were in the backyard throwing live charcoals at each other.

"Not a chance." I paused to collect more ammunition and pointed. "Maybe you would, Vic. Maybe. I don't know. Given Don's situation, backed against a wall, maybe most folks would fire away." I hesitated. "Hey Vic, I just thought of something."

"What?"

"The very fact that Don, an expert marksman, did not fire away at long-range, but waited until Blodgett was upon him, is big. Don't you think?"

"Yes. Maybe. The way I understand it, this was not a long-range situation. There was little time before Blodgett and Astin were upon him. A lawyer would know better than I."

"Hey, he didn't go shootin' the guy in the back either."

Monday, March 6, 2006

Yesterday I talked with Vic Blank, who has been the most proactive member of Team Graham. He called John Skowron, who immediately mailed Vic a copy of his revised report. Vic then called Gail Johnson and delivered a pep talk. He knows she's our best liaison to attorney Robert Mann. He's mailing Gail the revised *Skowron Report* and wants her to tell Mann to either come on board or at least lead us in the right direction. "I'm furious," Vic told me over the phone. "This would be a career case for Mann and we haven't gotten to first base."

"Welcome to the inner sanctum of the Donald S. Graham Obsessive Syndrome Club."

"It's driving me nuts. If we were younger, I might not be as affected by the element of time; but, at this stage of the game, every day is precious."

I needed to change the course of the conversation. "Haven't written in a week."

"What are you talking about?"

"I just haven't been energized."

"Are you blocked?"

"Hell no. It's a combination of things. This Achilles tendon is a pain in the ass. I'm finding there are 'time limits' to writing about morbidity. In other words, I need breaks now and then. And I've hit a temporary wall. Not a writing block."

"You'll be OK."

"I sure hope so."

"Did you ever consider writing this up as a series for a magazine?"

"Yes. What makes you ask?"

"Because, as a book, realistically, it may take another two years before you're published. And, like I said, time is precious." Vic paused. "And, with all due respect, it's not an easy task to get a book published."

"You're right, Vic, I fully agree. Twenty-two months ago, when I got underway with the project, I didn't have a clue as to what form of write this would be. I thought newspaper and magazine. Then, within two weeks I wrote up 44 pages. There were so many twists and turns that I realized the only way I could justify it would be in book form."

"That makes sense, I guess."

"And I'm no fool. I know how tough it is to get published."

"Stick to your guns, David. Keep banging away."

"Thanks Vic."

"For what?"

"I needed some inspiration."

"Good. Now get your ass in gear."

But I can't seem to get my ass into gear.

Woke up this morning, rolled off the bed, and stumbled into the bathroom on my crutches. That's what I do these days, roll and stumble. An active day concludes with blistered armpits.

Did my assigned therapeutic exercises, made coffee and sat down at my computer. I always begin by checking emails. Then I clicked onto www.adn.com/IDITAROD for updates on the race.

Was about to start writing. Instead I opened up "solitaire," and now it's nine at night.

I called attorney Robert Mann at 10 PM, March 10, 2006, his time. We talked for a half hour. He tried to open the program on his computer that would give him the Massachusetts Appeals Court opinion of the case. It wouldn't work. I finally got this guy to take action and his computer won't work. My acid reflux is in the boil-burn phase. He informs me he still hasn't had a chance to read the *Skowron Report*. Then, from out of the blue, he says, "By the way, I'm good friends with David Cooper, you know, my colleague who represented Mr. Graham at trial."

"Look, Bob, there are so many messed up points of law in Don's case that you don't have to attack on the basis of ineffective counsel."

He said he'd read the report and was willing to meet with Vic Blank.

Lately I've been getting on Maureen's case because she's always asking me questions. About everything. I've been brought up to pay close attention to questions. I don't have time for silly questions. They irritate me because I have to spend time addressing them. Questions about dyeing her hair or do I look like I've gained weight? C'mon, give me a break. These are questions of nonconsequence.

This happened yesterday. Maureen's driving, and a car is about to pull out of a side road. She asks me, "Is he going to pull out?" What am I supposed to answer? Then, she conjectures and asks me, "Supposing he did pull out and I avoided him … but the car behind me hits us?"

Who gives a shit? Who cares? This constant barrage of nonsensical questioning has a cumulative effect and then I get upset. I react by yelling and yacking at my dearest friend and loved one. A girl who never has bad intentions, who asks these questions innocently, out of habit. It's what girls do.

Mo's constant questions. Six weeks in a leg cast. Alaskan cabin fever. It's affected me as well as infected me. But most of all, an accumulated buildup of frustration and melancholia compounded from my Donald project. How do I best piece the story together? How do we get him out? The fear of not finding a publisher, knowing I must prepare a top-quality manuscript to succeed, and to succeed not only for me, but for Donald and his dear aunt, Agnes Smith. That puts my brain into a pressure cooker. So, when sweet Maureen asks me a foolish, innocent question, I lash out.

We talked about my verbally abusive reactions to her questions. She was surprised that I delved so deep into my psyche. Now, if she totally understands, she'll ease off. We'll see. I'm givin' 4-1 odds that nothing changes.

Mo went one step further in our healing chat. She made suggestions to the manuscript. "I think you should talk to Robert Astin; otherwise, the reader is going to feel short-changed by you overslanting the entire event in Donald Graham's favor. Granted, we both believe that Mr. Graham got a raw deal, but I think you need to hear from the other side."

Of course it's slanted. I'm writing about my friend. Mo's right. But how do I get to Astin? This has been bothering me for months. I always arrive at the same roadblock, the guy will never consent to an interview. Or maybe I'm hesitant, even afraid to confront him. Afraid of what I may hear.

I contacted all of Team Graham and asked them to come up with suggestions. What to do? How to do it? How to win Astin over?

Here's what the gang came back with:

1. Get as much background info as possible; even use a private investigator.
2. Find acquaintances of Astin and get suggestions.
3. Contact Blodgett's former wife for suggestions. She probably would be an ally.
4. Just call Astin. Get on the phone and do it. Be honest and say, "I'm calling from Alaska; have taken interest in the case and am writing about it, focusing on road rage; would be grateful for an interview."
5. Maybe a third party can set it up, like Victor Pichette, the private investigator hired by Don's defense counsel.

Cast removed today. My left leg does not look appetizing, more like a dry pork chop with hair on it. Reptilian. On the positive side, the doctor believes the tendon is repairing properly and will not require surgery. He explained this is a testy time, "be very careful, not too ambitious, or you'll be back here for another cast." In two days I start therapy.

Forget about attorney Robert Mann! I had a brief conversation with him and he flatly turned me down. He said, "I'm extremely friendly with David

Cooper. To go after David on the charge of ineffective defense counsel, is something I will not do."

This is after I definitively told him he doesn't have to attack on the basis of ineffective counsel because there are so many more approaches to the case. I just don't get it. Here we've spent gobs of precious time pursuing Mann and it turns out he's good buddies with Cooper. That's outright bad luck. Stopped me dead in my tracks.

Mann was kind enough to advise Vic Blank or me of other capable attorneys that may be willing to help.

April 5, 2006

An associate of Robert Mann contacted Vic Blank. She recommended a Massachusetts attorney. This is exactly what we don't want. A Massachusetts lawyer who cavorts with other brother lawyers, Massachusetts brethren, via a networking system that churns its way upstairs to the likes of Assistant Attorney General John Letourneau and Judge James McHugh III, the very prosecuting team that sentenced Graham.

Vic wrote Don asking him if he's exhausted his appeal options, state-wise and federally. And what would be the best cause(s) to bring about appeal.

Don responded on April 11, 2006:

Dear Vic,

The exact motion I would want an attorney to file to the Massachusetts Supreme Judicial Court (SJC) is a motion for a "writ of error." The error is the trial judge's (Judge James McHugh) error of altering his answer at trial (to defense counsel's objection to the entry of the tape recording of a portion of the charge to the jury) when he made his Rule 25 Motion ruling. The altered answer provided the basis for him to deny my motion for a new trial in my Rule 25 Motion and was also the basis for the SJC to rule against me. The SJC quoted the judge in his Motion ruling, not his statement at trial, when it ruled against me on this issue. I sent an affidavit to you that fairly cites what the judge did that was wrong, plus copies of the trial record and the altered statement in the Rule 25 Motion.

By tampering with the trial record of his own statement/answer to the objection at trial, the judge deliberately obstructed justice due me in 1996 to a new trial. His answer was on the same trial record page as was my counsel's objection, which he cited word for word. In his motion ruling he deleted his statements that my rights (to appeal) were saved. Then he added an instruction (in the ruling) that he had not made at trial: for counsel to renew the objection at the end of the instruction.

I may have another issue. On the night of 2/24/94 when the Woonsocket Police entered my house with drawn weapons, Sandra told them to "get out of this house with those guns." They told her to "sit down and shut up."

On 3/22/06 the Supreme Court ruled in Randolph vs Georgia

that police should not enter a home when one spouse tells them to leave, as Sandy did. Their entry, of course, permitted them to seize all the crossbows in my house, which were used as evidence against me at my trial and, as far as I'm concerned, greatly influenced the jury to convict me due to their perception that I was dangerous. The problem is that Sandy is not alive to offer an affidavit. I could write an affidavit, but the courts would probably disregard it as hearsay.

Anything you show a lawyer should include the earlier material I sent you. A trial judge is not allowed to change the trial record.

Lots of luck with Robert Mann!

Sincerely,

Don

Excerpts from a follow-up letter Vic received from Don:

4/14/06

Dear Vic,

Regarding my appealable issues: I have exhausted my state and federal appeals. As regards "statute of limitations," that term refers to prosecutable issues, not appealable issues.

In my last letter I told you I may have another appealable issue. Actually, I never invited the cops into my home. When the two Woonsocket cops came to my door, I stepped outside to talk to them. I took them to my car and showed them the taillight Blodgett had broken. They asked to see the inside of my trunk so I opened it and showed it to them. They asked about my crossbow and I told them I had taken it out and placed it in the storage area of my basement. I asked them if they wanted me to get it for them and they said yes. I returned to the house and went into the kitchen. I was unaware they were following right behind me with drawn guns and they followed me into the kitchen. That's when Sandy told them to get out of the house with those guns. They ordered us to sit down at the kitchen table while they secured the house. They ordered both my sons, Stuart and Stephen, at gunpoint, to go to the kitchen and then they searched the property. Neither of us agreed to the search at the time nor did we sign a consent form at the house. When Lt. Marzini arrived at the house, they asked if he had a consent form and he did not.

Later, at the police station, after giving a statement, I signed a consent form. My esteemed defense attorney, David Cooper, never inquired about the manner in which the cops came into my house. If Mann is friendly with Cooper, I don't want him.

I fired off a letter to Don requesting that he advise me about his years of alcoholism. Observing that the prosecuting attorney, John Letourneau, made such a big deal about vilifying Donald as an alcoholic, I wanted to hear more from Don on the issue. I just realized that during the time I knew Don, I never had a drink with him, nor did we ever talk about booze.

Don's reply:

4/19/06

Dear Dave,

It seems to be part of the human condition to repeat one's mistakes. I mention that as a caution. One stops making mistakes only when the problem is recognized and a conscious effort is made (daily) to break the "habit." One never knows when the opportunity to screw up will present itself, but sure as God made little green apples those opportunities will arise when least expected.

I have been free of booze since July 25, 1974, so did not have quite 20 years of sobriety at the time of the shooting. I have to be specific about that. I believe there is a genetic link, not just for alcoholism, but for most chemicals that affect seratin dopamine and other brain hormones that relate to human senses of well-being, euphoria, etc. These genes are linked and/or related in a complex manner that leaves a minority of people susceptible to addiction or uncontrolled usage, once begun.

I have read about a new drug that prevents the effects of alcohol on the brain from acting upon the release of these brain hormones, so that the use of these drugs will no longer give the user the sense of well-being. A user will still get drunk, however. In my opinion it remains to be seen whether this new drug is effective in treating chronic alcoholics.

1 know little about other mind altering substances.

I read somewhere that 10 percent of those who choose to use alcohol will suffer from its use. I am not saying those 10 percent will become alcoholics. Alcoholism is as unique as the individual, and at best, can be diagnosed best by the victim. Although it is diagnosable and treatable, one of the characteristics of alcoholic behavior is the ability of the victim to lie to himself about the nature and seriousness of his condition. It is a cruel paradox that the best diagnosis an addict can receive is his own self-diagnosis and that is prevented because it is the nature of addiction to deny the affliction.

My father, Frank Graham, spent a decade working up in northern Canada as a construction equipment mechanic. On one of his vacations he stayed at Ed and Agnes Smith's home in Petitcodiac. I was 14/15 at the time and recognized that he had a problem with alcohol. One afternoon he had opened a 40-ouncer of gin for a couple of swigs and then put the bottle under the sink to take downtown to the local pool hall later that night. Earlier in the afternoon he had killed another 40-ouncer. I took the empty bottle, filled it with water, and swapped it for the one he had just started with the water at the same level as the one with gin. Sure enough, he took the gin bottle full of water down to the pool hall to treat all the guys! He was not in an amicable mood by the time he returned to the house.

Dad joined AA shortly before he died of a heart attack at the age of 51 in 1964.

My knowledge of alcohol did not prevent me from using it later on in life. I had no problem in college and my use in this country was no great shakes. It was gradual and slowly increased through time. I probably crossed that invisible line in my late twenties. In 1968 I was driving my 1956 XK-140 Jaguar roadster and somehow found my way from Norwood, MA, where I lived at the time, to Woonsocket. I remember spending the night hitting the local bars and somehow misplaced my car. By the end of the weekend, I found a new place to live, on Oakley Road, and was eventually reunited with my car.

In 1969 I first attended AA meetings as well as group therapy at the Northern Rhode Island Mental Health Clinic on Hamlet Avenue in Woonsocket. I was honest enough to admit that I had a problem but could not see that my problem was unmanageable. That same year I began work in the paint department at the General Motors assembly plant in Framingham. I was drinking daily from 1969 to 1974 and can honestly say that I scarcely drew a sober breath in those years. As my bosses never saw me sober, they accepted me as I was.

In 1974 my shift was laid off when Iran doubled the price of oil. My wife decided to join the work force and got a secretary's job at Tupperware in North Smithfield. I stayed home and played Mr. Mom. My drinking became worse and one day I made pizza for the family but forgot to turn on the oven. Couldn't convince my three boys that raw pizza was edible. Gave them a real hard time about it. Sandy was not amused and put her foot down, hard. So I came to AA a second time. This time my sponsor was a fellow GM worker and I was forced to get honest about my condition.

I joined the St. James Episcopal Church group, also located on Hamlet Avenue, and have been sober ever since.

My marriage survived my drinking because I never cheated on my wife. I knew what she would not tolerate and that was one of them. Most women will not tolerate cheating no matter how open-minded they claim to be. It took me five years to "see the light." There are countless numbers of alcoholics with 50+ years of continuous sobriety and I hope to live long enough to join them ... about two decades to go.

From 1961 to 1971 I had five convictions of driving under the influence of alcohol (DUI). The last one put me into the House of Corrections in Billerica, MA for about three months on a six month sentence. The plant was on layoff when I went in and they let me out to return to work. That's when I stopped driving, but I had continued to drink for three more years. While I was in jail, Sandy moved from Oakley Road to an apartment on Park Avenue and had to go on welfare. Our boys were seven, five, and three at the time.

As mentioned in prior correspondence, to this day I attend my AA meetings. If the outside AA leader cannot make our prison meeting, I preside.

Take care, Dave,

Don

PS: I imagine you are glad to be out of the cast, as well as being in your own condo. Sounds like you really like Alaska. Permanently?

If medical malpractice could be proven, it could change things dramatically. So, when Dr. Martin Felder called today, I paid close attention.

As is his bent, Dr. Felder got right to the point. "I carefully read the testimony you sent me regarding the medical attention Mr. Blodgett received at Sturdy Memorial Hospital."

"What do you think?"

"I have one question. Do you know the reason Rhode Island Hospital refused to accept Mr. Blodgett as a patient?"

"From everything I've read, because of the two thoracic invasions."

"I see. That sounds right to me."

"Are we about to open a Pandora's box?" I felt a rash of tension creep into my anxiety.

"I don't think so."

"So?" My heartbeat settled down.

"If what I read is accurate, Mr. Blodgett was virtually DOA. His blood supply was already depleted by the time they arrived at Sturdy."

"Could they have done something else?"

"Yes. I wouldn't have performed the thoracic procedures. That could have been accomplished with a needle. But, in the whole scheme of things, I doubt if it really mattered. You see, so much brain damage had accrued, that had they somehow revived Mr. Blodgett, he'd be a virtual vegetable."

"Not good, any way you look at it."

"This is true. Stated differently, you'd have an engine running on empty."

April 21, 2006

Dear Donald,

An appellate attorney, Tom Dickinson (TD), has been recommended to us by Atty. Paul Cantor, Jeff Pine's partner. Pine is a longtime friend and former Rhode Island Attorney General; and, coincidentally, the AG of RI when you were sentenced back in 1995. Dickinson met with Vic yesterday. Vic gave him loads of material including the "Skowron Report." TD is already researching possibilities. He was not happy that so much time has passed since your conviction.

Vic gave TD your address and I think he will be in contact with you shortly. TD would only handle the appellate work. However, if he's successful in getting a retrial, it usually doesn't get that far. Normally a plea bargain follows. And with you already serving 10+, perhaps the judge will be lenient. Also, I doubt if guys like McHugh and Letourneau want to open any Pandora's boxes.

Oddly enough, Vic also got a call from Attorney Richard Egbert. He's high-profile; handled [Providence] Mayor Buddy Cianci's case. He'd be interested if your case went to trial. Told Vic to get back to him if there's need. That's an excellent ace in the hole.

Here's the rub. These guys don't practice for free. So this letter acts as a heads-up. Let Vic or me know if there is anything we can do.

Kudos go to Vic. He barreled right by Robert Mann and found some worthy lawyers. Dickinson has a good rep. Vic described him as an "honest engine."

The beat goes on,

David

I'm having a good day. Rare, I must say.

Ever hear of the "Nenana Ice Classic?" It's a lottery. Entrants, mostly Alaskans, try to guess the exact minute a wooden tripod sinks into the Tanana River. The tripod is set on a bend of the river in the city of Nenana, just south of Fairbanks. At some unknown moment during spring, the ice on the river will "break up" and the tripod sinks. The lucky winner is in for some serious bling. I feel like today is my "Break Up Day." My Achilles tendon continues to heal. Temperatures are rising. Fishing will commence within days. And most importantly, we're making a breakthrough on Donald's behalf.

Tom Dickinson called at 9 AM EDT, not knowing I was in Alaska, where it was 5 AM. I was half asleep. He's asking for a retainer and gave me an estimate as to what he expects his overall fees to be.

Donald is instructing his son, Stephen, to handle the financial transactions. Tom and I will maintain a running email dialogue, which is exactly what I was hoping for. Action. Finally. Feeling good.

I called Reverend Roger Francis in Florida. Roger referred to me as an "Angel of the Spirit." I've been called many things in my lifetime; "Angel of the Spirit" is not one of them. Not even close.

I replied, "Team Graham is a good team, Roger."

"Our combined spirits will carry the day."

Then I reported to Agnes and Ed Smith in New Brunswick, Don's aunt and uncle who took him in after his mother passed. Agnes was visiting a relative in Florida. Ed, who I had never spoken to before, dwelled on Donald's relationship with his father, reminiscing about his dissatisfaction with Frank for taking Donald's college tuition money for the purchase of a truck.

I then placed a call to Fall River, Massachusetts, the home of Christine Camara, the lady who allegedly had been abducted by Michael Blodgett. No dice, the number came up unlisted.

Tried reaching Victor Pichette in Rhode Island, the private investigator hired by Don's attorneys during the trial. A male voice came up on the answering machine. I asked Vic to call me back. A half hour later the phone rang and it was Lauren Pichette, Vic's wife. She informed me Vic's been in the hospital for three weeks with leukemia. His situation is not critical and Lauren thinks there's a good chance for full recovery.

She remembered that Victor was fascinated with the Graham case and promised to pass my message on.

May 5, 2006

Today's media focus is all about the World Trade Center tragedy of September 11, 2001. Yesterday, the trial of Zaccarias Moussaoui concluded. Moussaoui was one of Al Qaeda's major players.

Some of the victims' family members attended the trial and relived the horrors. The cockpit tape recordings of United Flight 93 were replayed for the first time. "I don't want to die," a passenger can be heard pleading, "I don't want to die." Tapes of emergency calls from the 83rd floor of the South Tower were replayed. "I'm going to die, aren't I? Please God, it's so hot. I'm burning up."

It strikes me as curious that both Moussaoui and Don Graham received the same sentence of *life without parole*. They'd make lousy roommates.

Placed a call to Paul LaRosa. Paul was the producer of the *48 Hour* special on road rage hosted by Dan Rather. Left a message on his answering machine. My goal is to get Paul to re-interview Robert Astin, with hopes he can draw out additional information.

LaRosa returned my call two hours later and we had a lengthy chat. He was very receptive to talking. The plan is for me to email him my request that he contact Astin.

I sent him everything in writing that I have on Astin along with excerpts from the *Skowron Report*. I asked if *48 Hours* would be interested in a follow-up program on Graham.

Early June 2006

Have emailed Tom Dickinson twice and left him a phone message. No reply. Nor have I heard from Paul LaRosa. Nor Scott Lutes, Graham's defense attorney. Nor Vic Pichette, Donald's private investigator. Vic Blank calls, Donald writes, and nothing else pans out.

Vic and Donald have been exchanging mail like grade school pen pals. They write about military books, contract bridge, chess, and the New England Patriots. They send each other Sudoku puzzles. Maybe, in time, Vic will request an adjoining cell.

On the flip side, of late, when Vic and I talk he expresses disappointment that Donald did not drive away. "How can a man so smart be so foolish?" he laments.

"Look, the fact is, he didn't. Accept it."

"I can't."

And each time I reply, "I know." Then I always conclude, "Vic, do you think he deserves life without parole?"

"Not on your life."

Chapter Seven

Vic #2, the Private Eye

I finally reached Victor Pichette on the phone. His voice sounded strong and confident, even though he'd recently returned home from the hospital. Leukemia at the age of 43, and he's on the mend. Vic is easy to talk to, he's not solicitous, nor contrary. He acknowledged that Don's case was by far the most interesting he's ever worked on. He also emphasized that attorneys Scott Lutes and David Cooper did an excellent job, based on what they had to work with.

"To work with? What does that mean?" I asked.

"You may not like what I have to say, but I'll be straight up with you."

"Good."

"I believe your friend was his own worst enemy. He made work very difficult for Scott and David. His lack of cooperation took up valuable time. Maximizing time is a huge commodity in the legal world. Like the adage, time is money."

"Are you saying if Graham had an F. Lee Bailey or an Alan Dershowitz, he'd be free today?"

"Let me finish. Maybe. I cannot answer that question. One thing we both know is that money talks. And I repeat, David Cooper and Scott Lutes did an excellent job on the Graham case. With what they had."

"That sounds pathetic."

"Sorry, but that's the nature of the beast. Donald Graham must have had limited funds. I was paid much less than standard fees and was somewhat limited in my parameters. I haven't a clue what he paid the lawyers. But, I know this, I went above and beyond, because I cared and wanted to. Maybe there are things that famous attorneys can do with beaucoup bucks, guys like Bailey and Dershowitz. Things we don't even know about. Then again, I'll stand by my statement that I believe his counsel also cared and extended themselves for Mr. Graham."

"Then why the hell didn't they win?"

"Like I said, I don't think you'll like my answers."

"Maybe. I know John Skowron didn't like many of the answers."

"I don't know John Skowron."

"You wouldn't, Victor. He's a longtime friend of Don's. He wrote a gutwrenching, sixteen-page report listing all the reasons Don should not be in jail. It might be biased, but it shows a lot of loopholes, and if Skowron's report gets to the right savior, it might free Graham."

"Well, he's still in prison, isn't he?"

"I'm afraid so. Anyway, let's get back to why I won't like your answers."

"Let me say this, there are some vitals to be understood when dealing with murder. First, you must understand the defendant gets one shot. That's it. Second thing is timing, the temper of the time. Back in 1994, road rage was a hot issue. That certainly was the case in New England. Hey, drive around Providence and by the time you get home, at least two hot-headed drivers will flip you the bird."

I laughed. "I know."

"Yeah, timing. Even preparation time is huge. The research, finding witnesses, braintrusting, prepping the client. Correct timing during the trial. When to ask a question. How to phrase it. On and on. And lastly, how to convince a jury. The impression a defendant gives to a jury. And ya know what, David?"

"What's that, Victor?"

"Donald Graham was his own worst enemy. I hate to say it, but it's true."

"You're right, I hate hearing this," I retorted, trying to defer his words; not sure if I could handle the criticism.

"And dammit, I like the guy. He's so smart and witty. The guy can talk on so many topics. He'd be a champion debater. He cares. He knows I like him."

"I'm sure he does."

"He always butted in. He gave the impression that he knew more than his counsel. I have lots of respect for Scott. He's a hard-working attorney. I know I keep hopping on that point, but it's meaningful. There would be times Scott and Dave Cooper would be onto something and Don would hold them back or not agree."

"I'm sure Donald's intentions were good," I interjected. "He's also totally honest, to a fault."

"Yes, no doubt. I found that out and it's another reason I was drawn to the man. At the same time, he had that 'holier than thou' attitude. He talked as though he did nothing wrong on that awful night. He made me feel if it happened again, he'd do it again. That's the impression he gave as a client and as a witness."

"I see."

"Hey, did you ever walk into a lawyer's office and see a picture of a large-mouth bass on the wall?"

"What?"

"A fish framed on the wall. I've seen that picture in several lawyers' offices."

"I think I understand."

"Of course you do. One of the first things a lawyer will tell his client is not to be the fish. Keep your bloody mouth shut."

"Do you have examples?"

"David and Scott would allow me to sit in on mock sessions with some of their clients, which I did for Donald Graham. I felt it was a privilege that they respected my opinion. It's a very important part of the process where the attorney preps the client for testimony. I always found this exercise to be the most fascinating and dramatic aspect of the entire procedure, like a rehearsal for a Broadway play. A most important exercise for Graham, because the guys didn't have much to go on."

"Can you explain that further?"

"Well, try to take an objective view of the case. It is true that Graham didn't know Blodgett from a hole in the wall. Graham initiated the action. He had the *atrocious* weapon stored in his trunk. And he shot Blodgett. Throw any slant on it you want, those are the basic facts."

"OK."

"During those mock sessions, Graham was uncooperative." Vic paused. "Noncompliant might be a better description. Most of the time he wouldn't go along with suggestions. He stood firm on his belief that what he did was not wrong. And the jury would see it his way."

"Really?"

"Really. And don't forget, there's only so much time. You're going to get one shot in a hostile environment."

"So going in…"

"Going in, I figured Graham was in deep doo-doo. The fact that he initiated the action by getting behind Blodgett and turning on his high beams displays premeditation. To a degree, it's not like he was in search of Blodgett for months and showed up that night with a loaded crossbow. Then again, the prosecuting attorney, Letourneau, portrayed Graham as a ruthless character with no remorse for his action. A one-man vigilante. He etched a precise description of Graham being an ace marksman. And Blodgett dies. If Graham was to get any edge, it might be because he had no previous criminal record, other than his DUIs.

It was important that Mr. Graham act humble in front of the jury. Hell, when you're up against first degree, it's a dire situation. Beg for mercy."

"I get your drift."

"You know the rest of the story."

The conversation stilled. Finally I asked, "So, bottom line, Mr. Pichette, do you think Donald Graham should be serving life without parole?"

"I knew you'd ask that question. First of all I don't know if he'll get another shot. I don't know if he's exhausted all his appeals. I do know if he gets that chance again, and I was the presiding judge, he'd have to act genuinely contrite, convince me of his remorse; that not in a million years would he ever pull such a stunt again."

"Thank you, Vic. I'm happy we got a chance to talk."

Victor Pichette didn't answer my question whether Don deserved life without. And he left me thinking what Don could say to satisfy a judge and at the same time be honest. Anything other than, "I am sorry. I would never do this again."

Is that honest? Could Don say, "As a man of conscience I am very sorry and I am remorseful. But please, put yourself in my shoes and understand at that moment of truth, as those two advanced, I was scared to death and filled with contempt because both my wife and I were so terribly threatened."

"But you put yourself in that situation," the judge might reply.

"But I never told those guys to leave their car."

Oh my God. This is driving me nuts.

I rifled off the following letter:

6/6/06

Don, greetings from the Last Frontier,

As I start my fourteenth month on the Graham Project, I must declare that it's been quite a broadening experience. Our exchange of letters. Talking with the likes of Colin Barrett and dear Aunt Agnes. The inclusion of Vic Blank. The intense interest people take once they hear the story. And, of course, the mission statement to get your ass onto free soil.

Today, I have mixed feelings. I felt very good about the hiring of Tom Dickinson. Then again, at this moment, I don't have a clue as to what he's done. At the outset he promised to keep me posted on his progress, and he hasn't. I expect you'll soon hear from Vic Blank sharing the same sentiments.

I've been affected by my recent conversation with Victor Pichette. He's in a struggle himself with leukemia and he truly strikes me as a good man. He'd love to see you get your freedom and sends regards. You know he's a straight-ahead guy and he believes if you get another shot, you MUST soften your stance. I've thought about his comments at length. It would be a compromise for you to some degree. Bottom line, I agree with Victor. If you need for me to be clearer, please say so. I think it's worthy of conversation. I was in a lull for about two months waiting for action to take place. Now we have action. Wish I could say the same about the first king salmon run, which is on hold. I've had one strike (in Homer two weeks ago) and did not bank the fish. It's all time sensitive — how's that for the proverb of the day?

Let's keep our fingers crossed. I sense we're getting close.

David

Attorney Tom Dickinson called, finally, apologizing for his lack of recent communications, explaining that he was busy with other cases (not what I wanted to hear). Tom reassured me he'd be visiting Don shortly and will keep me informed.

Tom got a kick out of us calling him TD, and closed by saying, "I hope to see you in the end zone." I liked that.

TD also spoke with Vic Blank today and indicated that, first blush, his primary thrust would be against the Woonsocket police for entering the Grahams' home without proper documentation.

I look forward to receiving Don's next letter. Curious how the deacon with the crossbow will respond to my constructive criticism.

A while back Vic Blank asked me to describe Don. His weight, height, what he's like. I remember saying that Don is adaptable. What an understatement. This guy has primal adaptive qualities. He can adapt to different environs. Prison has become his Sisyphean rock. He's developed a regimented discipline. He meditates and exercises. Eats three squares a day. The prison library acts as his learning chamber. He even champions a cribbage league. There's a TV in his cell. He has successfully built a viable cocoon. He's a professional adapter. The foundation behind Don's throne of adaptability is his faith. His faith that he will be a free man again.

June 20, 2006

Surprised I haven't received a letter from Donald. Figured he'd be quick to respond to my criticism. Maybe I overstepped my bounds and I'll receive no response. Think about it, who the hell am I? When's the last time I've been in a life-and-death situation? Like it's really none of my fucking business. Maybe he's written me off.

In the early going, shortly after Don and I began corresponding, Maureen sensed another side to Don. She was not taken in by his righteous attitude, his lack of remorse. I defended him to the hilt. Then there was the "no response" from his son, Stephen, after our only telephone conversation, when he promised to call back. Then, in the last few weeks, Vic Blank has felt a negative vibe, all about the crucial moment in "the incident" when Don decided to pull off the road behind Blodgett. That whole sequence is terribly flawed for Vic.

Now it's Vic calling, his voice ringing with optimism, the bad blister of angst broken. "Just got off the phone with Tom Dickinson. He had visited with Don and had an excellent first interview. TD still has homework to do, but he's rounding first base. Thinks he may have a shot by attacking the Woonsocket police who entered the Grahams' home without a search warrant."

"That's good news, Vic."

"Yes it is. I still think Tom should have gotten up to the prison sooner."

"Don's not his only client."

"I know. But he's *my* only client."

To wit, Don's next letter arrived with a postmark dated June 25, 2006:

Dear David,

I appreciate your mission statement, "to get your (mine) ass onto free soil." Seeing as America incarcerates a higher percentage of its citizens than any other country on earth, I suppose "free soil" would mean getting my ass back to Canada? I should be able to do that via international compact between United States and Canada. A life sentence in Canada is 15 years.

How many pages do you anticipate the book to contain at completion? Is page 242 near completion or halfway through? Have you considered doing two prologues for the book — me at age 23 and Blodgett at the same age, and what we were doing? Think about it.

Tom D. visited me a week ago. It was a good session. I've since sent him copies of my brief on appeal. I also have to get my trial transcripts ready for him to pick up. Waiting for them to allow me into the legal storage room to find them. Tom seems to be in his mid- to late-40s and he was not against my issue, re: Judge McHugh's tampering, but wants to get familiar with my case.

Can you send me Vic Pichette's address so I can send him a get-well card? He also struck me as a good man and a straight-up guy.

You wrote me that I must soften my stance if I get another chance. I hope to remain open to advice, but you never wrote as to what "issue" I am to soften my stance upon. I assume you save your letters on your computer, so whatever I have to soften, even at risk of compromise, please do some elaboration! I do need you to be clearer as I cannot always read between the lines.

The current issue of Field and Stream had a photo of a 60-pound king salmon. I can see why you are excited. We don't see fish like that in the Maritime provinces; at least not in my lifetime.

Sincerely,

Don

July 5, 2006

Dear Don,

You're 100 percent correct that I save all my letters on my computer. I'm one of those sentimentalists that saves most everything like beaten-up fishing lures to ballpark tickets.

I was surprised to hear that 15 years equals a life sentence in Canada. I could understand you wanting to return to Canada.

I'm not sure how long my manuscript will be. Depends on completion of interviews and what TD accomplishes. And I dearly would like to read the <u>complete</u> trial transcripts. I clearly see the light at the end of the tunnel. I'll take a shot and say 300 pages. Once I get done with first draft, I'll conduct a thorough edit; then, I'm ready for the next humungous challenge, which is to find a publisher. Networking helps in this area and <u>any</u> recommendation(s) is helpful. I've purposely held off sending the promo-pack to agents and publishers until I've completed the first draft.

I try to visualize the trial. Especially your participation. I reread the transcript from the "48 Hours" debacle. I reread the letter you sent me from Walpole shortly after your incarceration. Now understand, I come from a family experienced in the labors of salesmanship. I truly believe sensitive salesmanship is applicable in most every form of communication. Should be mentioned somewhere in the Ten Commandments. It is a Golden Rule.

Not for nuthin', Don, it's my humble opinion that you flunked salesmanship. You displayed a constant and bitter demeanor to the judge and jury. And with Dan Rather. One of no remorse. It did not work and will not work if we are to "set your feet on free soil" again. That's what I'm talking about. The worst part is that I know what was churning inside you, and being a contrarian myself, I'd want to throw a few hooks, but in the same breath when it comes crisis time, it's smartest to charm a grizzly.

I think to perfectly grasp what I'm saying, for you to gain harmony, you must look deepest into your soul at what happened that night and what you did. Whether Michael Blodgett was public enemy numero uno doesn't matter. Has nothing to do with guilty or not guilty. As I recall, dear Agnes shared with me a conversation you two had shortly after your incarceration in Walpole. I think she was trying to console you. "It was an act of self-defense," she said.

And you replied, "But aunt, I killed a man."

To me, that's <u>pure</u> acknowledgement of the <u>first</u> order. I respect the humility of the words and I forgive. I feel certain that a judge and jury would be of the same mind. Salesmanship.

Voila, I said it. And I'll stick by my guns. The door is always open to discussion or debate.

Sincerely, David

P.S. Enclosed is a note with Victor Pichette's address.

P.P.S. I'll be driving from Anchorage to Rhode Island in mid-September.

P.P.P.S. Enclosed is photo of a 58-pound, 48-inch king chinook I hammered on the Kenai River last July. Hell of a way to get a hernia.

Paul LaRosa, the producer of *48 Hours*, emailed me that he did not have the time to spend on our mission, and he reminded me that Dan Rather no longer worked for CBS.

I forgot that Rather got himself into a raft of shit criticizing President Bush's military career. Oh well.

Vic Blank mailed me part of a letter he recently received from Donald:

> Yes, I have a dim view of the entire legal profession in this country. When my trial judge tampered with the trial transcript of his answer to my lawyer's objection, he effectively retired the issue to the privacy of his chambers. There was no way counsel could represent me to a new instruction that was never heard by us.
>
> You must understand that, in my case, the appellate process is complete. Only <u>new issues</u>, or <u>new evidence</u>, can help me now. That is why I want to pursue the issue of judicial bias against me as evidenced by the judge (McHugh) changing his ruling.

Tough stuff. Leaves little room to maneuver. Tom Dickinson has his work cut out for him. Coincidentally, I spoke to Tom today. He was on his way to court. He's very busy and has not had a chance to pick up the trial transcripts. When I shared this with Vic, he became irate and will fax TD to treat Don's case with more urgency.

Don's letter dated July 17, 2006:

Dear David,

That salmon you caught last year must have been a once-in-a-lifetime experience! I see pictures like that in Field and Stream, generally catfish that big, but a salmon is something else. Atlantic salmon don't come close in size to that king.

Several weeks ago I got a set of trial transcript(s) for my new attorney, Tom Dickinson. He should be done by the time you come east in October, and I have no objection to your getting them from him. A copy of this letter should be satisfactory for him to give them to you.

It is very difficult to be a good salesman when on trial for your life, when you have no say in the questions being asked of you, when the State has provided a hero's funeral for a convicted pedo-phile, and denied me the use of his violent character to support my self-defense as guaranteed by the Supreme Court of the United States, and where the trial judge knowingly violated my rights to an unbiased jury. It's fine to be an armchair quarterback to assist in prevention of future mistakes at trial. I'm not too sure on how to charm a grizzly but am aware that some do it on a regular basis. There is still a big risk involved in that game, and it pays to keep some grizzly repellent handy. When these creatures turn on you, all the charm in the world is worthless. Seven or eight years ago a prosecutor in Worcester, MA said he could "convict a rock of first-degree murder, that's how easy it is in Massachu-setts." This was said at a Christmas party, and was reported in the newspapers. For the past decade (or longer) the Boston Globe has reported that the people of Massachusetts are the least charitable in America (according to IRS).

Blodgett's record, by itself, doesn't matter. But in a manner of defense of self and spouse, his record of repeat violent acts does have everything to do with my guilt or innocence, and the Supreme Court says so… But not the Massachusetts courts. When I told my aunt, "I killed a man," I was unaware of exactly where the arrow hit as I'd been partially blinded and thought I'd been wrong about the arrow hitting him high in the shoulder. It was later that I learned of the medical malpractice of the ER doctors. The arrow struck where a major artery is located and they failed to recognize that artery as the cause of all the external blood loss. He bled out, not in. They thought he <u>had internal</u> bleeding and wrongfully opened him up. Blodgett should have survived if they had treated the wound (correctly), which they never did in the first hour of treatment.

Judges and juries in Massachusetts are not in the business of for-giving, and never have been. The first white woman executed in America was hung in Harvard yard because she was a Quaker advocating peace with the local Indians.

My son Stephen had his first son, Stephen Aidan, and my first grandson in January of this year. First male in four generations without jug ears. Thank his wife for that!

Sounds like you plan to remain an Alaska resident. My sister Darlene lived on Vancouver Island for many years and loved it. But her daughter moved away! Kids.

Watching Martha (Stewart) and getting hungry!

Leave the grizzly charming to others.

Sincerely,

Don.

Vic Blank has played another card. Anticipating that attorney Tom Dickinson will have no grounds to appeal, he has delivered the *Skowron Report* to Joe Hopkins, a longtime friend, whose daughters are Massachusetts attorneys. On August 9, 2006 Merita Hopkins, one of the sisters, was sworn in as an associate justice of the Supreme Court for the Commonwealth of Massachusetts by Governor Mitt Romney. That's a high-profile position and her professional relationship with the governor might stand us in good stead for a *pardon*. Must play every card.

October 1, 2006 — Providence, RI

For the next three months I'll be residing at 28 South Court Street, located in the historical section on the east side of Providence. The second Rhode Island capitol building is across the street. George Washington spoke there, which means he slept nearby. At some point over the last few days, my footsteps traced those of the "Father of our country." I live within walking distance of Brown University, Rhode Island School of Design, and Johnson and Wales University. The famed John Brown House is around the corner on Benefit Street, as is Goeff's Sandwich Shop, which has the best half-sour pickles in Little Rhody.

It's good to be back home. I arrived on September 23 and have been on the go ever since. I've already spent time with my oldest son, Adam, and friends that I haven't seen since our departure almost two years ago.

Saturday (October 10, 2006), I received a surprise telephone call from Roger Francis, Pastor Emeritus of Don's church, the First Baptist Church of Woonsocket, where Donald served as a Deacon.

"How would you like to visit Donald with me tomorrow," Roger asked. He was in Massachusetts for a navy reunion. From a previous telephone conversation he knew I was in Rhode Island.

"Guess what, Roger. I was up there last week."

"I'll be darned."

"But I'd be delighted to go back."

"I'll meet you in the parking lot at twelve forty-five."

Maureen and the dog joined me, giving them the opportunity to enjoy the autumn New England foliage under clear, blue skies. That's right; our little pup is an Australian terrier, about as cute as a dog can be. We drove north on Route 95 and picked up 495 North; coincidentally passing by the exact spot where Graham shot Blodgett. We then headed west. I re-tracked my drive of a few days earlier. Roger and his wife, Isabelle, were waiting in the SBCC parking lot upon our arrival.

It had been nine years since I last saw Roger, during the *48 Hours* programming. I didn't recognize him. Back in the early 90s, when he was pastor of the First Baptist Church of Woonsocket, I had only met him once. And it's been all telephone conversations since. He looked older than he probably is, and that's because of a few injuries he's recently sustained, like falling off a canal wall in St. Petersburg, Florida. That misguided step damaged his hips (requiring surgery), his legs, and even caused some head injuries.

We signed in and followed the same protocol. "Take a seat and wait until your names are called," said the guard behind the desk. They made us wait a long time. I went out to the car to tell Maureen we still hadn't gotten in. She might as well go for a ride and return at three-thirty.

Back in the waiting room, I sat next to Roger. "Did I tell you that Donald has hired an appellate attorney?"

"No. I didn't know that. What's his name?"

"Tom Dickinson."

"Well, I hope for one thing."

"What's that, Roger?"

"That he's a man of conscience."

"I believe he is. He's worked for several attorneys general and comes well recommended."

"Thank God."

I knew that I had told Roger about Tom in previous conversations.

Finally at two forty-five our names were called. The same female guard as the last time conducted the shakedown. Roger failed the test. We were sent back to the waiting room and told we'd get another chance. We watched the three o'clock changing of the guards. Then the waiting room guard announced, "No more visitors."

What? I walked up to the guard and told him the good reverend had traveled to Massachusetts all the way from Florida just for this visit. And I'm here from Alaska. Don't know if we'll get another chance.

"Well, even if you get in now, you'd have less than a half hour."

"We'll take what we can get."

"Let's see what I can do."

The clock on the penitentiary wall read three-ten when we were seated in the visiting room.

Roger poked me in the side. "There's Donald."

He still looked good. He was in good spirits. "Nice to see you again, David. And Roger, what a surprise."

"Donald, you look good. Isabelle and I drove up for a navy reunion. I knew David was in Rhode Island, so I called him yesterday and here we are. The only bad part is that we arrived too late I'm afraid, and now we only have about fifteen minutes."

"We'll be OK, Roger."

The two of them small-talked for a few minutes. Don looked at me and said, "All of a sudden things are happening fast. I'm liking that. I've had one visit from Tom Dickinson. I think you found the right guy. Please thank Vic Blank. I've sent a letter to Tom. I know he's been busy with the Station fire case in West Warwick. I advised him what I believe to be the best avenue to pursue for appeal. And if that doesn't work, I want to be moved to Canada. In my home country, murder is, at worst, a fifteen-year sentence."

"But you're American and serving in an American prison."

"No, I'm not."

"You're not?"

"I never got American citizenship."

"What?"

"You didn't know that?"

"Not until now."

"It's true I was drafted into the U.S. military as a Canadian citizen."

"Does Dickinson know that?"

"Not until I told him."

"Did Lutes and Cooper know that?"

"Don't care to discuss them if we're down to eight minutes. Let's stick to new business."

There really wasn't any new business. Donald's agenda is set. He explained it to us:

A. One more attempt to overturn his verdict, focusing on Judge McHugh's tampering.

B. If that doesn't work, he wants to serve the remainder of his sentence in Canada, which involves negotiations with the Canadian Consulate.

So, we small-talked. Don asked if I was catching stripers in Rhode Island. He wanted details about our condo in Alaska. He was pleased to know our Rhode Island stay would last till mid-January and that I would revisit as often as possible. Roger and he chatted about the church and *Because He Lives*, and injuries. Then, the dreaded loudspeaker voice announced that we had to leave.

With the guards watching our every move, Pastor Roger Francis had us clasp hands. He issued a prayer. It was directed to Donald's freedom through perseverance and faith.

While shaking hands, I said, "Really wish we could stay longer. I'd like to take you on in a few games of cribbage."

"That might not be such a good idea. I take no prisoners around here."

On the drive home I tried to relive my second prison visit. I struggled in my attempt to remember the key parts of our conversation. I couldn't focus on details. I tried, but to no avail. I sat on every word, sentence, and paragraph back there in the prison. And now, when I'm supposed to be retentive, I've become inept.

Then, I realized I had the same problem during the drive home from my first visit only a few days earlier. Overwhelmed by the moment. External things I could remember, like the guilty feeling, the awkward "shakedowns," the waxed-floored corridor leading to the visiting room, how eerily quiet that walk was. I remember looking over at Roger and how we walked without daring to say a word. And finally the closely guarded visiting room, where we were not allowed to cross our legs.

Oddly enough, what I started to remember more clearly was my previous visit with Don, sitting in the Blue Section, listening intently, while he described the events of February 20, 1994. Both of us hanging on every word. I became a part of every moment of the tragedy, feeling the struggle of each character. And even now and perhaps forevermore, I can feel the shivery chill of winter air on that February night. Don's angst and ire upon spotting Blodgett and Astin lying back in the passing lane. How Sandra and he quaked with fear of a beating, the possibility of being killed. Don standing there in the open; Sandra numb in the front passenger seat. The sight of Blodgett's flashlight held upright in his large hand, its long, black, metallic lethality. The smashing sound when he smacked it on the back light of Donald's car. It no longer was a story to me, no wistful tale. I was there. I saw the crossbow. I felt Donald's shaky hands set the bolt. I could see that bolt flash through the air. The brief, hissing sound it made and the shocking feel of impact, as it hit and punctured Michael David Blodgett's shoulder. I could imagine that Michael felt warm blood pouring from the wound under his clothing. In short order I could vividly picture his lips turning blue, eyes glaze, mind wither, all ebbing life to a desperate end.

Chapter Eight

Legal Beagles

October 18, 2006

I picked up Vic Blank at his home in Cumberland. Seems like we talk on a daily basis, but I hadn't actually seen him in nearly two years. At seventy-five years old, my pal has gotten leaner and wrinklier. I expect most of that is from his bout with diabetes. He's still brimful of wit and fancy, and bent on Donald's freedom.

We drove over to the Dunkin' Donuts on Mendon Road to meet with attorney Tom Dickinson. Tom's a much bigger man than I expected, possessing a pleasant, round face with just a glimpse of aging; one that appears more defensive than prosecutorial. Tom was cordial, inquisitive, and businesslike. Very alert, a good storyteller, the type who needs little prompting to get the gist of any topic.

He's originally from Scituate, Mass., on the south shore of Cape Cod, where the ocean water is warmer than the frigid water's of the north shore. Tom and his family now live in Woonsocket. Just like Donald Graham, he found a bargain deal on housing. Prior to establishing his own practice, he worked for four different Rhode Island attorneys general, Dennis Roberts, Arlene Violet, James O'Neill, and Jeffrey Pine, who recommended Tom to us (actually, Pine's partner Paul Cantor recommended him).

During the last few months Tom's been spending most of his time on the Station fire case, a highly publicized pyrotechnic catastrophe occurring in a West Warwick, Rhode Island nightclub that resulted in the death of 100 victims. Tom represents one of the nightclub owners. The trial has now reached its conclusion. For most of the survivors and victims' family members, there will never be closure.

Hopefully, Tom will be able to devote more time to Don's case. He has the trial transcripts. Although he has yet to read the entire document, he's privy to the *Skowron Report* and clearly remembers most of the details. "Let me tell you for openers," Tom said, "I suspect we're dealing with a longshot here. Mr. Graham has already lost two appeals. For us to get action, we must present something new, something new and convincing. That doesn't mean we're dead in the water. It means we're playing on a shrunken playing field." At this point he ran a big hand across his evening beard, looked back and forth at Vic and me and said, "We have a hell of a challenge."

"I could tell from my visit with Don last week, he has an agenda," I replied.

"You're right about that." Tom reached into his folder and removed a letter from Don dated September 24, 2006. He read three of the paragraphs and handed the letter over to me as though I were a recording secretary. The paragraphs read:

> I strongly feel that my best chance for success lies with a motion for a Writ of Errors to the SJC (Supreme Judicial Court) to correct the trial judge's error in his written ruling to my post-trial Rule 25 motion for a new trial, based on the judge's sending, over objection, a tape recording into jury deliberations that contained only that part of the jury instructions that contained the charges for which I could be convicted.

> At trial the judge ruled: "I hear that objection and it is overruled. Your rights are saved in that regard." In his written ruling to my Rule 25 motion, the judge cited the trial objection word for word. The trial transcript of the objection also contained his answer at trial (above). The judge deleted the trial answer from his ruling and made up a different answer containing an instruction to trial counsel to repeat the objection at the end of the instructions: the judge effectively retried this issue in the privacy of his judge's chambers, without the presence of me, my counsel, or the jury. I see this action as a violation of the Massachusetts Canon of Judicial Conduct.

> I wish for you to address your efforts on my behalf to address the wrong done to me by this error. The question was never whether the jury understood the missing portion of the jury instruction. The question is whether the tape recording favored the prosecution's case. And it did. Each time it played further strengthened arguments for the jury to convict me.

"Don does his homework," Vic said.

"After last week's visit to the SBCC," I replied, "I've come away with the notion that if this plea doesn't work, he wants to make every effort to be transferred to a Canadian prison."

"Really?" Tom replied.

"Yes. Don never got his American citizenship. Always remained a Canadian. Funny, in his last letter he intimated that, but I misinterpreted the meaning. I thought he meant if he was ever set free, he'd want to return to Canada. Fact is, he volunteered into the U.S. Army as a Canadian."

"Maybe that can work in our favor," Vic said.

I continued, "If the petition you're to prepare, accusing the judge of transcript tampering, doesn't succeed, Don's next petition will ask to be transferred from the SBCC to a prison in Canada, with expectations that he would be set free after serving an aggregate of fifteen years, retro to day one served in Massachusetts."

"That's new news, isn't it?" Tom asked.

"Sure is. He served in the U.S. Army, in the famed 101st Airborne no less, as a Canadian."

"It's definitely an issue to pursue," Tom confirmed. "I have experience dealing with international consulates. I look forward to visiting with him again and getting details. Key is, we must make the right moves that will open the eyes of the appellate panel."

I said, "We fully agree. Meanwhile, I only hope that Don follows your lead. Gotta tell ya Tom, Don is a very steadfast guy, and may put up some resistance if you suggest deviating from his course of actions."

"I appreciate the advice. Could be that attacking the judge may not be the best approach. I'll certainly give his strategy consideration, and who knows, maybe he's right. But, first blush, my instincts tell me to attack on the basis of ineffective counsel, perhaps on several fronts. Another issue could be the Woonsocket police entering the Graham home without a search warrant. Nor did they obtain any signature from the Grahams. Apparently his counsel didn't pursue that."

I replied, "Vic and I have spent countless hours trying to conjure up new possibilities; maybe something that John Skowron didn't think of. For example, the lack of credible investigating at the scene. No taping off the area. No search for footsteps, blood, DNA, shattered glass from Don's taillight that was smashed by Blodgett — all of this could have changed the outcome."

Vic jumped in, "The fact that State Trooper Denise Adams was taken off the case and Trooper Ronald Blais, who recently died of cancer, was put in charge. Why?"

"Maybe an act of skullduggery," I added. "Perhaps Adams could shed light. Most everything written in the *Skowron Report* claims prosecutorial wrongdoing."

Tom said, "There's possibilities with Adams; but in the whole scheme of things, it's a stretch."

"Well, like you said, we've got to open a new can of worms," I replied. "Maybe the fact that Don's counsel did not bring credible witnesses to the stand." I pointed at both of them. "Hell, Prosecutor Letourneau portrayed Don as an ogre, an alcoholic, and a premeditating killer on a mission to murder Michael Blodgett. A few folks from church, maybe a witness or two from the 101st Airborne, would have portrayed a better persona of our friend."

Tom nodded. "I think that's going in a better direction. It's attacking ineffective counsel, and that may be our ticket."

Vic said, "I'm pleased we finally got this opportunity to meet. It's been a while coming and for a while I was worried that you were just too busy to put the necessary time and effort into Don's case. Now I feel better. Let me say this, I agree with David regarding Don's 'my way or the highway' attitude, but I also have come to know that he's a very bright man. He's reached a 'point of no return' status, and I'm confident that he'll respond favorably to your tactics."

"Let's hope so."

"One question, Tom."

"What's that, Vic?"

"Supposing you gain the attention of the appeal panel. That your arguments are so credible that a retrial is in order. Do you think Don's sentence will be overturned?"

"Based on precedents, my gut guess is it would never get that far. There's downtime and money involved in appeals, not to mention embarrassment, particularly in this case. Most likely, they'd decrease the sentence, and go retro. Your man could be free fast if we get to that juncture."

"That sounds good. One more question."

"Yes?"

"Based on what you know, was first degree / life without parole, the correct verdict?"

"I see this as a manslaughter conviction; possibly man-one or man-two."

As I drove home, I thought about "ineffective counsel." Both Paul Waldman and Bruce Krell, my lawyer buddies, proffered that same strategy several months ago. I also thought about Donald's defense counselors, attorneys Scott Lutes and David Cooper. Never did get a chance to converse with Cooper. But the few times I spoke with Scott, I heard the voice of a good, honest man, a hard worker. Must feel like shit to have an ineffective counsel charge brought against you.

I then thought back to my conversations with Victor Pichette, the private investigator. He was very open with me. He repeatedly complimented the work of Lutes and Cooper. He expressed his fondness for Don, and at the same time said he was not a cooperative client. I have mixed feelings. But the bottom line is the verdict. And for Don's sake I hope "ineffective counsel," if applied, would be effective enough to set him free.

Spoke to Vic Blank, who has recontacted Joe Hopkins to get a progress report. Joe has a copy of the *Skowron Report* and has hopefully passed it on to his daughter. Vic also advised Tom Dickinson of this move so that Tom stays in the loop. At this time Vic does not think Massachusetts Governor Mitt Romney would be responsive to pardoning Don. However, Vic does believe, and I agree with him, if Democratic gubernatorial candidate, Deval Patrick, defeats Republican Kerry Healey, Patrick may be sensitive to Don's case. If Judge Merita Hopkins, Joe's daughter, acts as an intermediary on Don's behalf, perhaps that might be the political punch to win the day with future governor Patrick.

Had another lengthy telcon with Victor Pichette, who I call Vic #2. He sounded good. He was energized to talk about my progress with the book. When I told him I visited Don at the pen, and how good Don looked, we both laughed. "That's ironic," Victor said, "I still remember when I first met Donald Graham. He was grim, gaunt and looked older than his age. Now you're telling me prison life is serving him well?"

"I'm not sure if it's serving him, but he never looked better."

"Not to change the subject," Victor said, "but I was just thinking about the first few times I met Graham. He had a non-Rhode Island voice, if that makes any sense, twangier. He had a stern and direct way. And I remember when I first asked him a few questions related to the case, his words echoed that if the situation arose again, he'd do it again if need be. I walked away and said to myself, this guy is cooked."

"Damn."

Victor continued, "I know. Funny, many people would applaud such conviction. Considering that his wife was in the car, it sure seems like a definable act of self-defense. I know you've done a lot of background search on this project, Dave, and that helps to understand the character. I've spent time thinking about that and I've come to the conclusion, on that awful night, Mr. Graham became a one-man vigilante. He became Charles Bronson in the movie, *Death Wish*. The soldier in him and his deep convictions merged. He spotted a rat and took matters into his own hands. Blodgett was evil and Don Graham stood for all that is good. Even if Graham had the chance to get away, he was as committed to making Blodgett pay as Blodgett was committed to kicking Don's ass. Turns out, Graham was better equipped than Blodgett."

"That's a mouthful, Vic."

"The flip side is that I like and respect Donald Graham."

"I know. I know."

"Like Jekyll and Hyde. You got one hell of a story there. Lots of open ends, twists and turns. I remember you asked me if I thought Graham deserved life without parole. Most likely not. But, if I were Blodgett's brother, even knowing that Blodgett was a bad seed, he didn't deserve to die that night. I'd want his killer put away for life."

Time marches on and I'm getting an eerie feeling that nothing is going to happen. The fact that the incident occurred over 12 years ago. That Donald is now 66. That he has lingered in prison for over a decade. Damn, soon we'll all be dead.

November 4, 2006

Dear Don,

I'm pleased to report that we have a new star member of Team Graham, Mr. Victor Pichette, who I refer to as Vic #2. We had a long chat yesterday, and this morning he called me with loads of information about Robert Astin — his address in Attleboro, and his telephone number. Vic even put in a call to the number and was told by a female that Astin was not home. I want to collect all my thoughts before contacting him. Make the timing right, give myself the best chance. Prevent the possibility of him hanging up.

I love how Vic #2 concluded our conversation. "Dave, it would be quite an accomplishment if we could reduce Don's sentence or set him free. Who knows what Astin may say? Who knows where his head is at? Maybe he's become a man of religion, a man of conscience. Maybe he's prepared to reveal facts that could blow open the case. One thing in your favor is that, if he sings, he's not in jeopardy. No way could he serve time for perjury at this point."

Vic also said, "I feel good that I've helped. After all, that's my job and that's what I was hired out to do." (P.S. Here's a guy with leukemia ready to carry the ball on fourth and long).

This has buoyed my spirits. Other than the addition of Tom Dickinson, it seems we've been on hold for a while. And now we're back in the hunt.

Of course, there's always the chance Astin may tell me to go fly a kite. That would be bad, but, you know, it's a statement in itself. And it's a step in the right direction. As Tom Dickinson said, the key is to find something new. This could be it. By the way, I've also found State Trooper Denise Adams who works out of the Foxboro barracks, and Wednesday I left a message on her answering machine. An interview with her could possibly provide new facts.

See you soon. Keep the faith.

David

November 8, 2006

Yesterday I drove back to prison. Constant rain and fog from Providence to the Neshoba Valley, which camouflages the Souza-Baranowski penitentiary within its thick forest. My car, a 1993 Chevy Cavalier station wagon, is great for fishing, but it's not geared for rainy weather. Somewhere under the accelerator and brake pedal is a mysterious leak and water seeps onto the floor. It's gotten so bad that in recent rainstorms I've had to bail.

I was better prepared for shakedown this third time around. Emptied my pockets before leaving the car. Had a quarter ready for the safety deposit box, where I stored my wallet and car keys. And, to while time away in the waiting room, I brought along *The Providence Journal,* which was filled with bylines regarding the national Democratic landslide in last night's off-year elections. Deval Patrick won the governor's seat in Massachusetts.

Passed my shakedown with flying colors. The female guard who rejected me the last time complimented my preparedness. An electronically controlled door slid open and I walked down the long corridor of the inner sanctum. The floor was still perfectly waxed. Along the way I looked through a barred window and could see the prison's outer wall with circular barbed-wire at the top of the high fence. There was a space of maybe 30 feet and a second inner fence stood closer to the building. The ground was covered with groomed gravel, reminding me of a major league baseball park's warning path in the outfield. Once gaining entry into the visiting room, I noticed there were fewer visitors this time. Weekdays are less crowded than Sundays.

A hefty young woman dressed in too-tight jeans sat off to my left with her convicted husband. He looked like a tough hombre, eyes constantly shifting around the room, as his wife nervously talked. And she did most of the talking. Another prisoner, sitting to my right, had to be 80 years old, the spitting image of Ghandi, especially with the bare-rimmed glasses. He had an elderly female visitor.

A woman and her two young children sat in front of me. The kids were playing with crayons and a coloring book. When the prisoner arrived, his wife had to restrain the kids. This inmate looked like a movie star with black, shiny, perfectly combed, long hair, like Antonio Banderas. The way he ran his fingers through his kid's hair broke my heart. What brought him to the big house?

Donald arrived at one forty-five. We'd have plenty of time to chat. We covered a lot of territory. We talked about his First Baptist Church of Woonsocket. Don said it was built in 1898. Lots of tradition. He mentioned old-time church member names like the Youngs and Buntings. Don reminded me of a vandalism insurance claim and how pleased the property committee was with the way I handled it. He wanted to know all about my visit to the church with Pat Dempster and how *Because He Lives* was doing. He was delighted that the soup kitchen was bigger than ever, and Pat was as energetic as her husband Paul had been. We shared stories about Paul Dempster.

"Don, tell me about your father."

He paused, held his hand to his face for a moment, and then emphatically stated, "My father was a man of many qualities, both good and bad. Nothing subtle or quaint about Dad. Always knew where he was coming from. He was a big guy, much taller and broader than me. The outdoorsman-type who lived to hunt and hunt. An amazing shot. I think I told you he was reputed to be one of New Brunswick's finest deer guides. Problem is he was hardly around. Most of the time my dad was in faraway places doing surveying work for highway systems."

"Did you hunt with him?"

"Never. I wasn't interested. I just liked archery. Shooting at targets was my game." He glanced at the guard station.

We somehow got to talking about "Beaver" Tempest, another illustrious Woonsocket tragedy, whose murder trial took place around the same time as Don's. Beaver also got first-degree for allegedly killing a girl in the basement of her apartment building. What made his case so electric was his father, who was the chief of detectives for the Woonsocket Police Department. Another son, Gordie, served on the Woonsocket PD. And yet another son, John, was a longtime friend of mine. The whole affair became highly publicized. The greatest irony is that Beaver, like Donald, worked in the paint department at General Motors in Framingham.

Don said, "Beaver struck me as a bipolar type of guy. Never knew which personality would show up for work. Always got along fine with him. I know his family is still trying to prove his innocence." Don paused and grinned. "That GM paint department sure produced some Hall of Fame alumni, eh."

I asked if Tom Dickinson had visited recently.

"Nope." Don seemed nonchalant, *ennui* in his tone.

"You seem unconcerned. I'm very concerned."

"Sorry, my mind is all over the lot. Believe me I'm concerned. You know I've written him and given precise instructions as to what I want him to pursue."

"Yes, I know that."

"After considering everything, I believe the tampering of testimony by presiding Judge McHugh is the way to go."

"I hope so. I do know, Tom is keen on the issue of the Woonsocket Police not getting you to sign a Consent Form to enter your home."

"That's OK, but not what I want." He almost jumped out of his chair. "If we keep dancing around minor issues, the appeal board will take another five fucking years just to acknowledge our argument. Listen David, I know the best course to follow. Maybe Dickinson is too timid to go after the judge, because it's so incendiary."

I raised my hands.

Don raised his hands. "In which case I've blown more money bringing him on board."

"Hold on," I countered. "Dickinson has solid credentials. He's served under four Rhode Island attorneys general. He served under Jeffrey Pine, who was Rhode Island attorney general in 1995, the year you were sentenced."

There was a long pause. Don's eyes rolled. I knew he was thinking that TD has the instincts of a prosecutor. Just like David Cooper, his first attorney. Now his odds seemed further reduced. Don stared at me. "Fucking lawyers. If only I was in a Canadian prison, I'd only have to serve another three years."

"I feel awful. Look, Dickinson was highly recommended and I played a role in getting him, and he might not be meeting his fiduciary responsibility. Maybe I should ask for your retainer back."

"Maybe he will help. Maybe there's credibility in pursuing the Woonsocket police. Maybe Officer Jack Marzini could help. I understand he's retired and living in Florida."

"We could find him."

"Maybe."

"If it proves important, we'll find him." I said, "Ya know, I'm influenced by what both Dickinson and you said regarding *new* facts — that that's how we can reopen the case. With the help of Victor Pichette, we've found Patrol-woman Denise Adams and I've placed a call to her at the Foxborough barracks."

"You mentioned that in your last letter. I suspect when Patrolman Ronald Blais relieved her of her duties, his assignment was to suppress my case. And that's why the investigation at the scene was so shoddy. No trace of footsteps, no broken glass, and so forth. Meanwhile, Blais died, but if Denise kept notes, that could open up *new* inroads."

"I should be able to get to her."

"Good. I'm thankful for Victor Pichette's help. I pray for him."

"He's handling his bout with leukemia like a champ. And Victor found your friend, Robert Astin."

"You're a real comic, David. With friends like that, who needs enemies."

"I have not tried calling Astin yet. I'm hesitant…"

"It would be a miracle if he came clean."

"That's the idea. What was Astin like?"

Donald hesitated, as though he didn't want to answer. "A big guy, taller than Blodgett."

"I thought Blodgett was six-foot-six."

"No, not at all. Blodgett was five-ten and 265 pounds. He looked like a rhino as he came at me. Astin's about six feet, and he prevented me from retreating because he got behind me."

"Why didn't he jump you?"

"Good question. My guess is he could see the crossbow and was scared shitless." Don paused. "What was he like, you ask. He was Blodgett's buddy. He probably had the power to convince Blodgett to give up the chase, but he didn't. He was also given the opportunity to change his initial police report three times, three fucking times, until the fourth report was satisfactory as far as Prosecutor Letourneau was concerned. He's a snake in the grass as far as I'm concerned."

"If I could just get him to cooperate with me. I'm still trying to figure out the best approach, the best timing."

A loudspeaker sounded, interrupting our exchange. Visiting hours were over. I checked the clock on the wall, confirming it was three-thirty. There was more to talk about. I looked at Don forlornly. "That's it."

He nodded.

We watched husbands and wives, boyfriends and girlfriends, romantically embrace. I said, "Well my friend, again, no kisses."

"We'll survive that one."

Walking back to the waiting room, I felt miserable, visualizing Don in a shakedown cubicle, removing his clothing so prison guards could make sure he didn't have a hidden weapon or a bag of some hideous drug hiding in his ass.

I drove home with the steady beat of rain falling on my soggy Chevy Cavalier. Never turned the radio on. I did leave a message on attorney Tom Dickinson's cell phone asking him to get in touch with me ASAP. It's been nearly a month since we met. I feel like a micromanaging watchdog, or as Don describes Vic Blank, "a border collie."

TD never returned my call. So I called him and he answered immediately.

"Look Tom, this whole affair seems to be getting worse, especially after visiting Don last week. And I'm bothered that you didn't return my call. Maybe you're too busy. I don't know. It's driving me nuts. It's time to shit or get off the pot."

"Take it easy David."

"Look counselor, we need to feel your passion. What we need is for you to be our hero. Or you know what?"

"What?"

"You can quit the case."

"That doesn't seem to be the goal here."

"Maybe you're too busy."

"I must get up there."

"That's an understatement, Tom. Look, I need to get together with you, lots to go over, especially since my visit to the SBCC."

"Do you have anything new?"

I quickly thought about Victor Pichette, State Policewoman Denise Adams, Ronald Blais, and Woonsocket's Officer Marzini. "I've written every-thing down."

"I'll call you tomorrow. Should be able to work something out for Thursday. What time is good for you?"

"Anytime. It's your call."

"I'll call you tomorrow."

"Sure hope so. Thank you."

What the hell am I thanking him for? He's got a retainer and Don's still in jail.

Lawyers. These privileged few, who call each other "brother" in a court of law, but will cut each other's throat in a New York flash for some self-serving agenda that might have nothing to do with their client. Which reminds me, this past weekend we saw a movie called *The Departed*. Hell of a cast, Jack Nicholson, Matt Damon and Leonardo DiCaprio. Massachusetts is the setting. All about policing and twisting, cheating, stealing and killing.

I'll reserve my final grades for Mr. Dickinson. I'm dying to see him come through in the clutch. The very thought of having to go out and find another lawyer is discouraging as well as time-sensitive.

For the first few days I was delighted to be back in Rhode Island. Granted our living quarters in Providence are sparse, but that's easily compromised with all the wonderful history only footsteps away. Like the Rhode Island School of Design Art Museum, great Italian restaurants in the Federal Hill district of Providence, College Hill, and cruising the streets of my Woonsocket childhood.

Then again, so much has changed that I no longer feel like I'm a homegrown Rhode Islander. Last week while in Woonsocket, I had the emptiest feeling. Most of my acquaintances have either moved on or are dead. And there are parts of Woonsocket that are so built up, they've become unrecognizable. Surrounding towns seem to blend into one, each losing its singularity. Most everywhere seems more dingy and congested. City districts that were filled with tradition, ethnicity and character have become concrete jungles.

I hate to be so depressing. Maybe it's just the temper of the month, which has been filled with rainy, gloomy days. It's even screwed up the fishing and will probably sink my Chevy Cavalier.

November 15, 2006

When it comes to driving an automobile, Vic Blank coined the expression, "an accident ready to happen." He's had so many fender benders he should be honorary president of the Assigned Risk Pool. So I picked him up at his home in Cumberland, left the Chevy Cavalier in his driveway to dry, and drove his van to the SBCC. Vic had never been to a prison before. Finally, the pen pals would meet.

I introduced them in the visitors room of the SBCC Blue Section. After a few brief exchanges, Don gave a shortened rendition of the incident. Vic couldn't resist asking, "Why didn't you pass Blodgett and get the hell out of there?"

And Don again explained that he was "afraid to get in front of the guy," that he was better off behind him. "That way I could at least know what his next move would be. And remember, I was driving a beat-up jalopy."

Vic talked about the Hopkins daughters, especially Merita, the recently appointed judge. "I'm afraid she's turned us down."

"I suppose if she did get involved," Don replied, "it would create a conflict with Thomas More Dickinson, whom I've already retained."

"I know," Vic said. "I was hoping Merita Hopkins could lead us to Governor Deval Patrick for a possible pardon."

"Not a good shot," Don replied, "seeing the last pardon in Massachusetts was given to Willie Horton in 1988. Once released, Willie went on a rape rampage. Anyway, you know my feeling about lawyers and turning my hopes to another Massachusetts lawyer-turned-judge, who probably has some type of relationship with Judge McHugh, as well as Letourneau. I'm very leery. I appreciate your effort Vic, but I think I'll stick with Tom Dickinson. For better or worse, that's who I'm banking on."

"Well, TD seems to be a problem," I jumped in. "He was hired in April and he's moving at a snail's pace. I don't think anything has happened since Vic and I met with him a month ago. That's driving me nuts."

"Driving *you* nuts?" Don reddened. "How do you think *I* feel? He knows exactly what I want done. Nothing complex, very simply attempt to overthrow the appeal based on McHugh's tampering with testimony, or get me up to Canada.

"It's a dual-edged sword, isn't it? I'm banking on him and he seems to be procrastinating. Lawyers."

"He hasn't returned our calls."

"I have no problem with David and me acting as border collies," Vic said, "but nothing happens unless Tom moves."

Don said, "So much for turning to other counsel. Like I've told you earlier, going after McHugh is incendiary. If I can get the verdict overturned, McHugh could lose his judgeship. I could think of no better gift. Look, just find out if Tom's ready to move on this. And would he please get up here as soon as possible."

"I'll try reaching him again on the drive home," I promised.

A young, bald-headed prison guard approached Vic and told him to un-cross his legs, and instructed me to remove my arm from behind Don's seat.

"Fucking twirp," Don whispered as the guard moved on. "Mark Twain once said, 'If you want to see the scum of the earth, be at a prison during the changing of the guards.'" Don straightened his eyeglasses. "I know this guy and he thinks he's an Alcatraz TV star. Truth is, he's a first-class prick. Most of the guards are OK." Don paused and slipped a peek in the direction of the guard station. "You cannot begin to imagine what a prisoner and visitor will cook up to exchange drugs in this room."

Vic tried to suppress a laugh. He turned to glance at me and winced from the arthritis in his neck.

Donald continued, "The Canadian option, by the way, is not a bad one, you know. If Tom has experience dealing with consulates, I definitely want him to proceed in that direction. But most of all, I need him up here."

"We'll do our best," I replied. "By the way, Don, I've been meaning to ask you about Blodgett's suspended criminal records. Those copies you mailed me. Are they official documents?"

Donald frowned and replied curtly, "Look, don't believe me. Ask Victor Pichette. He uncovered Blodgett's record."

Vic quickly changed the subject by asking about prison life.

I'm listening, and at the same time berating myself for asking the criminal record question. I interrupt, saying to Don, "Did anyone ever tell you, you look like Gordie Howe?"

Quickly recomposed, Don laughed, comfortable that I changed the subject. He explained to Vic that Howe was a former, great Canadian hockey player for the Detroit Red Wings. "Howe's a lot bigger than me. Of course now that I'm at 185 pounds, I'm catching up."

Vic commented, "From your photos and now that we've met, I swear you're the spitting image of Billy Bob Thornton."

"Yeah right," Don replied. "And when David gets his book written, Billy Bob can play my role and win an Oscar." Then Don pointed out another convict sitting behind us with a young woman. I had noticed him earlier because of his features. He was older than most of the other inmates, about Don's age, and stood out. There was an ambiance, an aura about the guy, tall, straight, authoritative. He had a pleasant, almost honorable look. "That's Billy Baronski. He's in for life. The young girl is his daughter. Billy was one of Whitey Bulger's honchos. I like Billy. We play cards together."

"Does that mean he was a hit man?" Vic asked.

"I don't know. You'd have to ask him that."

For the first time in my three visits I began sensing what it must be like behind bars. Till now, I never actualized Don as a convict, refusing to accept the reality, like living in a bad fantasy. Now, hard truth and reality set in. My friend had assimilated into the inside and gained respect from his fellow convicts. Being a former alcoholic, a card player, jailhouse lawyer, and lifer, Donald had gained upper-crust status. I figure most of his fellow inmates felt he had performed an honorable deed in dismissing Blodgett.

After retrieving our wallets and keys from the prison safety deposit box, we began our return drive to Rhode Island. I asked Vic, "How are you feeling?"

"Seven."

"Not bad for a hypochondriac."

"You're a wise guy. You should know better than to mock the infirmed."

"OK, OK. I'm curious, now that you've heard Don's side of the story, does it make more sense to you that he pulled in behind Blodgett instead of trying to drive off?"

"Yes, it does." Then he jabbed me in the arm. "Yes it doesn't. My immediate reaction, my first thought is always, why the hell didn't he just get outta there?"

I smiled. "I understand and I suppose I agree. Seems anyone in their right mind would have aborted. One thing for sure, though, it initiated the last act of the tragedy."

"Yes it did."

"And although it's questionable and irrational, pulling off the road behind Blodgett makes a little bit more sense now."

There was a lengthy pause in the conversation. I broke the silence. "Well, Mr. Blank, what are you taking home with you?"

"How precious freedom is."

After dropping Vic off, I managed to reach Tom Dickinson and set an appointment with him for tomorrow afternoon.

November 16, 2006

What concerned me most about Tom Dickinson's office in Johnston (RI) was the enormous piles of files on his desk. For a big guy, he appeared dwarfish surrounded by the paperwork.

I reiterated Don's priority, that he was dogged in his approach to go after Judge McHugh for tampering with testimony. Again, TD was not receptive to that strategy. "That's a common approach, especially for convicts who've been in the can for a long time, revenge against the judge who put him behind bars."

"But there's merit in the approach."

"It's old business. It's been used in previous appeals."

"So where do you suggest we go?"

"At this point I still like moving against the Woonsocket police not procuring a letter of consent."

"Don seems to think that Lt. Marzini could be helpful on that one. He thinks Marzini moved to Florida."

"We could find him if he still exists. Like I said, I think this is our best shot."

"How about getting Donald up to Canada to complete his term?"

"That's another possibility."

"Don seems to think it's a good shot," I said. "Fifteen years is a maximum sentence there, for any crime."

"Well, it's not all that simple. Don't think for a minute that Massachusetts would release him without constraints. There has to be a treaty between the two countries or between Massachusetts and New Brunswick, something like that. And I think there is." Tom began hitting keys on his laptop and shortly said, "There is. I'll have to take a closer look."

"Good."

"Don't get too excited, and don't forget what I told Vic and you at Dunkin' Donuts."

"Everything's a long shot."

"Correct."

"I don't know, Tom. Don is so adamant about attacking the judge. On one of my visits, when I asked for more details, he got mad at me, telling me it's all spelled out in the trial transcript, reminding me that McHugh overruled defense attorney Cooper's objection regarding the incomplete tape, regarding criteria to sentence, regarding the fact that McHugh prejudiced that tape by only explaining criteria to find Graham guilty of first-degree."

"You're spot on."

"That's the way I understand it, that McHugh told defense counsel Cooper to save the objection for later in the trial. Then, after the trial, on his own time, McHugh tampered with his very own words, changing the transcript. Don just about yelled at me, 'It's all black and white; anyone who eats food can see that.'" I took a deep breath. "You're not afraid to go after the judge, are you?"

"Hell no."

"Why did McHugh overrule the objection and then tell him to save it?"

"I can't be sure."

"Cuz the entire system was trying to railroad Donald?"

"That's conjecture."

"That's bullshit. This whole fucking case stinks. Bottom line, no one, not one person I talk to, thinks he deserves life without parole. Please help, Tom."

"I'll get up there."

"Sounds good to me, counselor." I looked at the stacks on his desk. "When?"

He looked at his appointment book. "Things are slowing down a bit."

"You can do better than that."

"Next week is a short week. Thanksgiving." He paused. "Maybe Monday."

"I'll make the drive with you."

"You can't go in with me."

"I'll stay in the car and drive back with you and listen."

"I'll give you a call."

I shuddered at the thought. "That would be excellent. Anything else you can think of, Tom?"

"Not at the moment. How about you?"

"Well, I still remember how you emphasized to Vic and me that anything *new* could work. With that in mind I've found Denise Adams."

"The state trooper?"

"Yes."

"Where is she?"

"Still working out of the Foxborough barracks. I've left two messages."

"And she hasn't replied, right?"

"Right." We both smiled. "But I know that her shift begins at 3 PM, and I plan on going up there tomorrow."

"To accomplish what?"

"Well, that can be part of our conversation on Monday."

"I'll give you a call."

I feel like a private investigator. Or a sneak. Drove up to the State Police barracks in Foxboro. Hadn't been in that neck of the woods in years. For me Foxboro is interesting for two reasons. One, it domiciles the New England Patriots, and two, I cannot figure out if the town is spelled Foxboro or Foxborough. I think the residents are also confused, because around town I saw both spellings.

Foxborough is about a half-hour drive north from Providence. The barracks is located on historical Route 1, also known as the Boston Post Road. My objective was to meet Massachusetts State Trooper Denise Adams. An attempt at a sneak approach.

Expecting she'd arrive around three to begin her shift, I pulled into the adjacent parking lot at two-thirty. I hunched low in the driver's seat, hoping to see Trooper Evans drive into the parking lot, at which time I'd spring from my mildewed Chevy and charge the front steps of the barracks. Then, I'd start asking questions. Instead I stared at the quiet barracks, a two-story, red brick building with both an American and POW/MIA flag blowing in the wind. Shortly before three, the clouds broke and the sun came out, which I figured might be the harbinger of good luck. But, when the clock struck three, no Denise.

I walked into the barracks and asked for her. The trooper behind the glass window advised me she was out on the road. "Would you like to leave her a note?" He explained that the normal procedure is to call in and set an appointment. He said he'd put my note in her mailbox. So I printed out my name and telephone number and asked her to please call. For the third time.

On the drive home I took Interstate 495 to 95, and shortly after gaining access to 95, I drove by the location where Don shot Michael Blodgett. I could not identify the exact spot, because it's a shoulder off the road, not a rest stop. It still felt spooky. This was about three twenty-five and the traffic was horrific.

Shortly after returning home, Denise Adams returned my call. I explained to her that I was in the process of writing a book about the Graham/Blodgett encounter. She immediately acknowledged the incident and said she'd be willing to answer questions. She gave me her fax number and address.

Our conversation was pleasant, professional, and brief. Before hanging up I asked her, "Do you believe Mr. Graham deserved a verdict of first degree, life without parole?"

Without hesitation she replied, "Absolutely."

Monday, November 20, 2006

Talked with TD today. I was hoping he'd tell me we'd be driving up to Shirley this afternoon. Instead he confirmed that we wouldn't. "But maybe Friday. I'll let you know on Wednesday."

Not the words I wanted to hear. I told him about my brief encounter with Trooper Denise Adams. Then I said, "Tom, I have an idea. Not sure if I can explain it perfectly, but I know you'll understand."

"What's the idea?"

"I think in legal terms it's called a proffer. Supposing you contacted the Massachusetts Board of Appeals. Or Judge James McHugh, directly. Tell him that you're confident that you have two issues strong enough to grant a retrial. Hold back on what the issues are. And barter for Don's release to Canada."

"I'll give you credit for trying, David."

"Thanks. Look, if they insist on knowing the issues, then sock it to them. Maybe it would scare Judge McHugh and they just might bite and take your proffer to avoid any embarrassment."

"In my legal career, I've never seen such a maneuver work."

I considered his comment. "Hey, there's a first time for everything."

"I suppose. Look, I think it's good that you're in there swinging. And don't stop. As soon as possible, I must look further into getting him to Canada."

"Now you're talking."

"And I know you're dying to get me up to Shirley."

"Oh yes."

"Hopefully, on Friday. I'll call you Wednesday."

"It'd be one hell of a Thanksgiving gift."

November 22, 2006

State Trooper Denise Adams
136 Washington Street
Foxborough, MA 02035

Dear Denise,

Thanks for your return call. I think I mentioned to you that I'm a resident of Anchorage, AK. I'm here for another month and then return home. As a former New Englander, I've been aware of the Graham/Blodgett incident since its inception and have always felt it to be an incredibly tragic, compelling, and sad story. I've tried to put myself in your shoes on that dreadful night. It had to be a difficult ordeal.

As a work of non-fiction, it's vital that I present this story clearly and honestly. I'm a believer there are three sides to every story, and let's face it, this one could have more. Below are my questions:

1. Can you share your initial reactions?

2. Can you describe Graham, Mrs. Graham, and Robert Astin?
   What they were like?
   Did you feel more sympathy for one or the other?

3. Did you spend much time at the scene of the crime?
   Did you take notes or tape-record?
   How and why did Trooper Blais get involved?

4. Did you attend the trial?

5. Did Trooper Blais or you know either Mr. Blodgett or Mr. Astin prior to the incident?

6. Have you seen or talked to Mr. Astin since the incident?

7. Are there any additional, unknown or noteworthy facts you can share with me?

8. Have you read the *Skowron Report?*

9. Is there anyone else you suggest I talk to?

Also enclosed you'll find a preliminary draft of the incident. If you find any inaccuracies, I sure wish you'd advise.

On behalf of my research team and myself, I'd like to thank you in advance for your help.

Sincerely,

David G. Brown

Encs:

January 2, 2007

Mrs. Agnes Smith
301-50 Cameron Street
Moncton, New Brunswick
Canada EIC 9A9

Dear Agnes,

Happy New Year.

It's been almost six months since I received your letter. Thanks for sending the many photographs. I am keeping seven and returning the rest per your request. I've closely looked at all of them and see a spiritual commonality in each of you; a strong sense of family. Makes me feel great. At the same time, it breaks my heart. Hopefully, these photos will appear in a published book entitled *Deacon's Crossbow*. Hopefully.

Have been on the move of late. Spent four months back in Rhode Island from October to this January and just arrived in California, where we'll remain till mid-April. And then we'll drive back to Alaska. My new address is: 512 Apple Creek Lane, Santa Rosa, CA 95401.

While I was home I visited Donald four times. Compared to the photos you sent me he has put on weight and I think it becomes him. It was an excellent opportunity to catch up on many things. My greatest impression regards his ability to adapt and making the best of any situation.

I did little writing in Rhode Island. Not sure if that's good or bad. It's bad because I want to complete my manuscript yesterday and I still think there's another fifty pages to go. That all depends on what happens next. I do know that the appellate attorney we've hired was terribly slow in starting up on the case. And that put me on hold. Thankfully, he recently visited Donald and is now underway in preparing Donald's next appeal. Technically, it's a tad more complicated than that. Suffice it to say, a plan is on the drawing board to gain Don's freedom. So, that's GOOD news.

Oftentimes I think of Ed and you. It's like I'm up there in Moncton. I feel the strains and pains of octogenarianism. I feel like I experienced Donald's growing-up years.

I know that faith keeps Donald going. I'm envious of that. I do know that it's vital for all of us to stay busy, take care of each other, and hopefully this challenge will have a satisfactory ending. I hope I see the day when Don's giving you a hug, Agnes.

With love,

David Brown

February 1, 2007

Never received a response from Trooper Denise Adams.

October 9, 2007

Vic Blank just called. "A supreme court judge, his name is Spina, the justice assigned to review Don's case..."

"Yes."

"He turned down the petitions for retrial." Vic's voice was solemn. "Bang, just like that."

Even knowing our chances were slim, even preparing for this, his words slashed painfully like the thrust of a bayonet. I kept repeating to myself Vic's words, "Bang, just like that."

"David, are you there?"

"Yeah, I'm here."

"I'm sorry. We've tried so hard. I feel just awful. Very helpless at this point."

"I know. I guess we better do some hard thinking."

"I'll talk to you soon."

As soon as I hung up, I wondered what difference any of this makes. Whatever we do, we lose. Lose, lose, lose, lose. I could picture Don sitting on his bunk, reading the decision. I could see him staring through his cell bars, looking up, wondering about faith.

I emailed the following to Tom Dickinson:

> Dear Tom, As you might imagine, I'm downhearted. Vic gave me the basics pertaining to the denial; however, I don't fully grasp how the decision came down. Would you kindly forward the paperwork and advise anything else I should know. I think it would be good for you to visit Don ASAP. He could use the morale boost. I hope your heart and soul remain with this challenge. I'm certain TIOTE. Regards, David

October 10, 2007

I'm shaving. Looking in the mirror I see a face that embodies the agony-of-defeat look. I ask the face, "Why the hell are you so driven? Why can't you just give up? Why let this affair take you down so?" I stare at the face. "Shut up and don't cut yourself."

Something's terribly awry, fundamentally wrong if you believe, as most people I've interviewed do, that the verdict and sentence was wrong. It seems as though Judge James McHugh III, Assistant District Attorney Letourneau and the Massachusetts judicial system have total control over Don's destiny. I'm thinking about Tom Dickinson's comment how cons seek revenge against their judge, like Robert Mitchum in *Cape Fear* – his anger and hate, his vicious quest for revenge. It makes sense to me now that anything related to Massachusetts in Donald's case is a lost cause. A wall. They have everything locked up and have thrown the key away on my friend.

Seems to me the direction, the focus, has to go back to Rhode Island. Maybe best to pursue the "no search warrant" by the Woonsocket police; or, as many have suggested, "ineffective counsel."

What's the next move?

October 22, 2007

Not a freaking word from Tom Dickinson.

October 30, 2007

I received a call from Bruce Krell, my San Francisco attorney friend. I told him about Judge Spina's ruling on the two petitions. "It doesn't look good, Bruce. Apparently the entire supreme court panel will follow up on Spina's findings and then they'll all render a final decree."

Bruce replied, "Well, that panel is the Massachusetts Supreme Court. You know, Mr. Graham still has the right to appeal to the U.S. Supreme Court."

"Yes, I know. Odds are about 1,000 to 1."

"I'm afraid you're right about that."

"I feel awful."

"Listen, never give up hope. I know the energy you're expending. Keep going. Don't stop. And who the hell knows what rewards your book will bring? In thirty-seven years of practice, twice I've utilized words from books that helped me win cases. The public word and sentiment can be a major influence in the judicial world. Keep going, David. I certainly believe your cause is justified. Something will break."

October 31, 2007

Wasn't sure if it was trick or treat when the phone rang this morning. It's the Souza-Baranowski Correctional Center. I hear a recorded male voice giving a long list of instructions. I'm advised this is a collect call. The call may be recorded. I'm asked to give my credit card number, along with several other prompts, and then, finally, I hear, "David?"

"Donald?"

We both laugh. I ask, "Have you ever called Alaska before?"

"I'm surprised I got through. I thought you could only get smoke signals up there. Listen, there's a chance that the entire supreme court panel will overrule Spina's decision and recommend retrial." A trace of optimism coursed his voice. "As a rule, these decisions are made in short order. I'm counting on the Canadian petition for relief due to consular rights; that is, not getting a chance to seek legal help from Canada, my home country. This relates to an ongoing trial in Texas," he explained. "A Mexican defendant, who, like me, was not given his consular rights, awaits a decision from the United States Supreme Court. If he's granted a retrial, that would set a precedent for my case."

"Aha, that is encouraging."

"Yes. Supposedly even President Bush has put his two cents in the Mexican case. He's lobbying for a retrial. So, we'll see. We might know in a week. I sure hope so. Tell ya one thing, Dave, we'll read about it in the newspapers, that's for sure. As soon as they drop the gavel."

"Interesting. So we sit and we wait."

"I've become very good at that."

"Hey, the bases are loaded. We need a base hit." I could picture him standing there at the phone booth, probably a guard nearby, maybe another inmate. Don in his faded orange jumpsuit, the yellowed sneakers.

He replied, "I have faith. The books of Job and Ecclesiastes say it best."

"It does, huh? I ain't the most religious guy in the world; but, if need be, I'll climb Mt. Denali and do a rain dance."

"That's a high mountain."

"Whatever it takes, Don, whatever it takes."

"By the way, congratulations on becoming a grandfather."

"Thanks. It's a hell of a feeling. Ya know, I'll be seeing you around Thanksgiving. I'm coming home to see the little guy. Hopefully, Vic Blank will join me for the ride."

"That will be nice."

"It will. Meant to tell you, I had a long chat with Victor Pichette and he's in total remission and back to working full-time as a private investigator."

Before Don could reply, the recorded voice returned, "You have sixty seconds remaining."

"Oh shit," I said, "didn't expect that. Is there anything urgent to discuss right now?"

"No. No time right now. See you next month."

"Yes. Meanwhile, Vic and I have been talking about finances and I know you'll be receiving a letter addressing that issue. He mailed it today."

"Very good. Give Maureen a hug for me."

"Count on it." His voice was replaced by a droning buzz.

I mailed out a short note:

> Dear Don,
>
> It was good to hear from you. There was more I wanted to talk about, like Agnes and the funeral she recently attended in Massachusetts. Wanted to discuss your son, Stephen, because there are money issues, which I know Vic will be addressing shortly. And I have preliminary thoughts about former attorney general Jeff Pine as a potential candidate for your legal counsel.
>
> Regards,
>
> David

November 1, 2007

At 9 AM my telephone rings. I pick it up, and hear the same recorded voice as yesterday from the Souza-Baranowski Correctional Center. All the same instructions. Yesterday's call from Donald was the first, and now another one within twenty-four hours? Something hot has happened. Maybe the supreme court has rendered its final decision.

The voice is shelling out instructions. I'm trying to be attentive, I press a number on my phone per the voice's prompt ... and I lose the connection. All I hear is a dial tone. Why was Don calling? Maybe he'll try again. Must stay near the phone.

November 3, 2007

Don never called back.

November 25, 2007

The Thanksgiving week flight from Alaska seemed endless. Three legs: from Anchorage to Las Vegas. Vegas to Pittsburgh. Pitt to Providence. The worst part, I don't sleep on planes. Everything ached when I stumbled onto Rhode Island soil at T.F. Greene Airport.

Went to the cemetery to visit my parents' graves. They lie next to parents and brothers of the Brown family. And the gate was locked. On Thanksgiving. It made no sense. So, I stood on the sidewalk, peering through the steel fence. It was bizarre, standing so far away, but I did feel an at-oneness with three generations, now that baby Cole is on board. My God, I thought, my mother would have adored this kid.

I lingered about, looking through the fence and spotting gravestones of so many people I knew, bringing about so many vivid and varied memories, like standing in front of Peter Macktaz's grey, marble stone. I could picture his broad frame, his winning smile and laugh, his *joie de vivre*. I had forgotten that his middle name was Yale. He was three years older than me. We were in Boy Scouts together. Played sports together. Peter entered law school at Suffolk University when I was an undergrad and leaving. We'd drive into Boston to see Bobby Orr's Bruins games. Our kids grew up together — and now Peter's gone.

I was awed by lots of names. Maynard Ginsberg, who fought in the First World War and told me frontline stories about dodging machine-gun fire and marching through French fields filled with poison gases. I could see the stone of Dr. Saul Wittes, our family doctor, who flew planes over Europe during World War II. I grew up with his son, Bobby. We all fished together. Saul delivered me. Seems like my parents' entire generation lay under that grass. Walking back to the car, I felt that Alaska was planets away.

Thanksgiving morning I attended the annual Woonsocket vs Cumberland high school football game at Barry Field in Woonsocket, a trip down memory lane. During my high school days, Barry Field is where I practiced and competed in track. And hockey as well, when a corner section of the field was frozen in the winter. On that ice in 1957 I managed to break my knee, osteochondritis disicans of femeral condyle. I looked at those words on my cast for eight weeks. Good old Barry Field, where so many Woonsocket kids experienced the joy of victory and the agony of defeat. My favorite memory of all was a simple game of catch with my childhood hero, Clem Labine, who pitched for both the Brooklyn and the Los Angeles Dodgers. His throws were so hard that the ball made a hissing sound. Clem died a few months ago at the age of eighty.

On a cloudy, drizzly Wednesday afternoon (November 21, 2007) I picked up Vic Blank at his home in Cumberland. We visited Don at the Souza-Baranowski Correctional Center.

Arrived at 1:45. All the same protocols. We filled out the same entry forms in the waiting room, placed all our extras in the safety deposit box — keys, wallets, hats, my copper wrist band. Same twenty-five-cent charge. During shakedown Vic was sent back to the waiting room — twice. First he forgot to remove a ring, then he forgot to remove a necklace. By the time we arrived in the Blue Section of the visiting room, it was two o'clock. The inmates were wearing gray jumpsuits. All with the large D O C printed on their backs. Not many visitors. Maybe Thanksgiving is a time where friends and relatives shy away from prisons?

Don was wearing a smile as he passed the guard desk and joined us in the exact same seats as the last time.

Most of the conversation revolved around Don's attorney, Tom Dickinson, who has a deadline of November 27, 2007 to respond to Judge Spina of the Massachusetts Supreme Court. Spina has ruled to deny both motions for re-trial. Our biggest concern should be Spina's denial; instead, we're all bothered because Dickinson has not kept us up to date on his progress with the response. We crave to know that counsel is working with the same urgency we feel.

So we game-planned. Jeff Pine's name was thrown on the table.

I thought back to Dickinson's hiring, via the recommendation of attorney Paul Cantor, Jeff Pine's partner, and an acquaintance of Vic Blank. I played no role in that decision. Never took the time to research, reference, and meet Tom. Next thing I know, Donald, through his son, Stephen, sent a retainer to Dickinson. That was close to two years ago. And we're still diddling. I cannot allow this to happen again.

We also discussed finances. Don was unsure how much was in his bank account, which is overseen by his son, Stephen. We felt it important that

Stephen be contacted in the near future. I could sense uncertainty on Don's part, that maybe some rift existed.

"Most importantly," I said, "we need answers, as soon as possible, so we know how much dough we have to play with. What's the next move? Whether we're in a position to replace Dickinson, if it comes to that."

We all nodded. It occurred to me to ask Agnes and Ed Smith to make contact with Stephen. Or perhaps Pastor Roger Francis could make the call. Knowing this to be a touchy subject, Vic completely changed directions. "Do you think you'd be better off in another prison? One that's not maximum security like the SBCC?"

"This is the place for me, Vic."

"It is?"

"It's the only Massachusetts prison with air conditioning."

Vic smiled.

"I'm dead serious. A/C is big on steamy summer days. Another thing, I have a large cell compared to other joints. I have no cellmate. Think about that one. Supposing the guy didn't like me. I could be stabbed in the middle of the night. Or supposing he just went nuts." There was a moment of silence. Don opened the palms of his hands. "Who knows what could happen?" He glanced at Vic. "I'm OK right here."

Then I asked Don why he called me again on the day after our Halloween phone conversation. "It's been driving me nuts for pressing the wrong prompt and promptly disconnecting us." I wanted to apologize.

"I never called you back, David."

"You didn't?"

"I'm tellin' ya." He thought for a moment. " I bet it was the prison. I think they make random callbacks for security reasons, or some such bullshit. But, rest assured, it wasn't me."

At three twenty-five a guard announced we had five minutes to leave.

We leave. Don stays. Vic and I are free. Don has one option — after his shakedown he must return to his cell.

Chapter Nine

Back to Alaska

Coincidentally, the prison movie, *Shawshank Redemption,* premiered in 1994, the very year Don Graham encountered Michael Blodgett. The final scene of the movie has Red (Morgan Freeman) rendezvousing with Dufresne (Tim Robbins) on a sunny tropical island surrounded by tranquil aquamarine seas. It brought to mind a song I've listened to throughout the years, elegantly sung by bluesman Leon Redbone.

DREAMER'S HOLIDAY

Climb upon a butterfly and take up on a breeze.
Let your worries flutter by and do the things you please.
In a land where dollar bills are falling off the trees;
on a Dreamer's Holiday.

Everyday for breakfast there's a dish of scrambled stars
and for luncheon
you'll be munchin rainbow candy bars,
you'll be livin' ala mode on Jupiter or Mars,
on a Dreamer's Holiday.

Make it a long vacation.
Time there is plenty of.
You'll need no reservation.
Just bring along the one you love.

Help yourself to happiness
and sprinkle it with mirth.
Close your eyes and concentrate
and dream for all your worth.
You will feel terrific, when you get back down to earth,
On a Dreamer's Holiday.

Words by Kim Gannon

Sunday, November 25, 2007

The first telephone call I made upon arriving home in Alaska was to the good reverend emeritus Roger Francis to discuss Don's financial situation. Hadn't spoken to Roger in a while and this would be a chance to play catchup. Also on my mind was an earlier conversation we had, over a year ago, when Roger offered to call Steve to play a more proactive role in his father's cause. So, I called in that favor, but Roger was not home. I left a message on his answering machine.

I then placed a call to Agnes and Ed Smith. They were very agreeable to discussing the financial situation with Steve. Agnes indicated that Stephen was her favorite nephew and she should be able to gather all the necessary information. Hopefully, we'll get the results quickly.

Roger Francis returned my call. I told him that Agnes was taking on the job and I'd keep him posted.

Wednesday, November 28, 2007

Agnes and Ed have yet to call back.

Thursday, November 29, 2007

Have heard nothing from Tom Dickinson. Vic called asking if I heard from Agnes. He also wanted to know if I heard from Dickinson.

Why can't we catch one bloody break?

December 24, 2007

Dear Don,

In the 12/4/07 Opinion Section of the Alaska Daily News, there's a syndicated article written by Derrick Z. Jackson of the Boston Globe. It's about U.S. District Court Judge Nancy Gertner and how she pardoned a small-time crack dealer, Myles Haynes, after he served 13 months of hard time. The gist of the article relates to drugs, racism, and insufficient rehab for prisoners.

The article piqued my interest because Jackson is trying to convince us that Gertner is a liberal, who has compassion for the incarcerated. I have a copy of Roger Francis' letter, written on 1/21/01, to Judge Gertner, asking for her help on your behalf. She never replied to Roger (that's what he told me). To wit, I prepared a draft letter to her. Instead of mailing it right out, I'd like you to review it and make any suggestions or corrections. Maybe there's no gain in even sending it. Why did Roger plea to her instead of another Justice?

I'd like us to speed up our actions, and maybe pursue more than one target — like a plea to the governor; or, sending a promo-pack to a few TV programs. Or asking the help of Judge Gertner.

In talking with Agnes last week, I wanted her to know that I am especially careful treading in another family's business. In all due respect, I have Stephen on my mind. From the one time I spoke with Steve, I sensed there were issues, and I understand issues. Usually there are three sides to every story. For all I know, and it's not much, Stephen may have total justification to hold you in contempt for something(s). Bottom line, regardless of Steve's gripe, he's handling your money, and I believe he's obligated to let you know how much is in the till. I expect Agnes will be calling Steve soon.

Regards,

David

The draft letter:

Dear Judge Gertner.

Recently, I read an interesting article, printed in the Anchorage Daily News and written by Darrick Z. Jackson of the Boston Globe. The article was about you. The subject is Myles Haynes, his exploits and his recent release from prison, due in part to your effort(s). A story loaded with misfortune, irony, and leniency. It indicates to me that you are a woman of compassion.

I must share with you that I have a longtime friend, Donald S. Graham. He was a client of mine when I owned an insurance agency in Woonsocket. Donald was valedictorian of his high school class, served in the 101st Airborne, a father and husband, and deacon at his church. Presently, Graham resides at the Souza-Baranowski Correctional Center in Shirley, serving a life-without-parole sentence. Donald is referred to as the "Route 95 Crossbow Killer."

I've spent the last 2½ years writing a book about this tragedy. Hopefully, it will be published soon. With the help of "Team Graham," we've collected a tome of information. Graham is a fascinating story.

What's coincidental is that I have a copy of a letter written by Pastor Emeritus Roger Francis to you dated 1/21/01. In short, it was a request to reopen the Graham case. It was a plea for help.

Pastor Francis is a man of undying conviction and a great guy. If you met him, you'd love him to death. Never in a million years would he have written to you if he wasn't certain Donald Graham's sentence should be reduced. And I agree. At this stage of the game, he could still be making a contribution to our society. And I believe the taxpayers of Massachusetts are wasting their money at their expense to keep Graham behind bars.

Judge Gertner, can you help? I'd be extremely thankful if you replied.

Cordially, David G. Brown

January 12, 2008

Mr. Robert A. Astin
49 Augsburg Drive
Attleboro, MA 02703

Dear Mr. Astin,

I'm researching the Michael Blodgett and Donald Graham incident.

My heart goes out to you for having such a traumatic experience. There are a few questions I'd like to ask. I fully understand if you do not want to respond. But, if you do, I'd like to know what went on in the car as you drove from Route 95 to Sturdy. What you remember and what you felt.

Thank you,

David Brown

March 4, 2008

Have not received a reply from Judge Nancy Gertner.
The January 12, 2008 letter I sent to Robert Astin has been returned to me.
It's almost eight o'clock in the evening on the east coast. Just left a message on Jeff Pine's cell phone. Expected Jeff wouldn't answer. But that's OK, my message said it all. Both Vic Blank and I believe that Jeff, as a former Rhode Island attorney general, loaded with political savvy, would be the perfect counsel for Don. Don concurs. So, I called.
Here's what's puzzling me tonight. Most everyone agrees that Don's sentence of first degree / life without parole is a shafting. But, when I try to enlist the help of Rhode Island's most noted criminal defense attorney, then Don's son, a television producer, a Massachusetts state cop who was involved, a newspaper reporter, and most everyone else, I get no help. Right now, I'm feeling very alone, and my guy is simply going to fade away into the woods of Shirley, Massachusetts.

Sunday, March 9, 2008

Based on Vic Blank's call today, Jeff Pine will be put on hold.

Don's attorney, Tom Dickinson, called Vic yesterday with the news that the Massachusetts Supreme Court has agreed to meet with Tom on April 8, a mere month from now, to discuss the two motions. Vic did not know all the particulars. Tom mentioned the court has allotted a ten-minute session.

"Well, it's better than nothing," Vic said.

"Absolutely. And, who knows, maybe it'll last longer."

"Conjecture."

"I know, but not out of the question."

"I'm sure I'll get more details and I'll pass them on to you."

"Thanks Vic. I'm encouraged."

"I know. This could be very exciting, or it could be nothing."

"I think I'll send an email to TD tomorrow."

"Good idea."

March 10, 2008

Dear Tom,

I'm encouraged by the news Vic Blank delivered yesterday about the upcoming April 8 hearing with the Massachusetts Supreme Judicial Court.

Here's a thought. It has to do with the presiding judge, James McHugh III. If the Supreme Court sends the case back to the Superior Court for a decision, won't it be tainted by the fact that McHugh serves on the MA Superior Appellate Court? It seems to me he'll do anything to squash the case. Just one of many issues that keep me up at night.

I wish you the best of success. Is there anything I can do to help? Would it be helpful to recruit a bunch of Donald Graham's backers in the audience? I'm sure I could round them up from Donald's church.

Cordially, David Brown

As usual, Vic Blank's been corresponding with Don. The emphasis of recent exchanges concerns the Massachusetts Supreme Court's offer to meet with Tom Dickinson on April 8. We're not even positive what they want to talk about. Most probably, they will address the two motions. Maybe all the complaints about collusion, bias, and altering issued in the first motion has gained the interest of the supreme court. Or they'll question Motion 2, regarding Don's return to Canada. Maybe the Court agrees that Don did not get his Vienna Convention rights.

Who the hell knows? Prisons are overfilled today. Perhaps Massachusetts wants to unload Donald, although my San Fran lawyer friend, Bruce Krell, thinks that applies only to minor offenders.

To my way of thinking the best-case scenario is if the court recommends retrial and Don is given the opportunity to cop a plea, most likely based on "time served." The boys sit down around a round table, parley, and Don is released because he's already served 12½ years. It is possible, it could happen.

Now Don is claiming he will not cop a plea. Excerpts from his letter to Vic dated March 16, 2008:

Yes. I am 100% certain that I can make an argument to have the indictment dismissed, as the prosecutor perpetrated a complete fraud on the grand jurors. He withheld the four police reports of Det. Berard (Attleboro), Trooper Adams (State), and Woonsocket Police(two reports) from the jury and didn't let them know those reports existed because they had a different version of events than what the jury heard. He also withheld a death certificate with a different cause of death than the one seen by the grand jury. He allowed false testimony as to Blodgett's criminal record. He allowed false testimony as to medical procedures performed on Blodgett at Sturdy Hospital. He gave a motion to the court with the false statement that Blodgett's record never became part of the case.

As far as "time served," that is an admission of guilt. If set free,

I would not be able to set a free foot in America. I'd be taken in chains from SBCC to immigration and put on a plane, cannot file for social security, and do not collect social security $. Don't know if one can apply for benefits by mail, but suspect not. First things first. I need SJC to order a new trial, or dismiss indictment.

Oh my. I'm having trouble with this. My first reaction is, "cop a plea." Set yourself free. Then, if you want retribution, do it from free soil. I see the chance to gain freedom as more than a vendetta. I see it as a matter of life and death. There's no shame in humbling oneself, if that's what it takes to go home. Lest we forget, Donald did kill a man. Forget about all the extraneous bullshit. Michael Blodgett died that cold February night without benefit of a trial.

However, I also know about Donald's pride along with his righteousness and belief that he justifiably acted in self-defense. I admire this tenacity, but his pride and conviction could keep him behind bars forever.

March 23, 2008

Dear Donald,

I'm sweating bullets over this April 8 meeting with the Massachusetts Supreme Court. I believe the best result would be a retrial. If so, this could provide you the opportunity to cop a plea, probably based on time served.

At first I wanted to write this letter advising you to cop the plea. I know that's Vic's recommendation. I spoke with Agnes and Ed and they feel the same way. I suspect most folk would agree. I love thinking that Donald S. Graham can be free. I want to transcend those words from thought to reality. It means we could fish together; I could whoop your ass in cribbage.

Then it occurred to me that I have no right to be invasive. This decision is yours. Therefore, this letter serves as notice that whatever you decide to do, I support unconditionally. Period. I have always admired your principles and undying faith. That combination should provide the correct decision.

Funny, I cannot pray for you, Donald, because I don't pray. But, I am so convinced that your sentencing was wrong, I will rely on faith. That you will be served.

Cop a plea — take a retrial? Again, I support your decision and envision the day when Agnes can give you a hug in Moncton.

Sincerely, love and peace,

David

April 8, 2008

Rolled around in bed till 4 AM, at which time I walked over to Jerry Nagle's home to watch the Massachusetts Supreme Judicial Court hearing scheduled for 9 AM Eastern time. Amazing, through an online link with Suffolk University, they televise appellate case hearings. I'm 5,500 miles away. Fifty years ago, to me, Alaska was another planet. Now, I live on that planet and can watch Don Graham's fate unfold on a computer screen.

Turns out that it wasn't until 12:21 PM when Docket #10074 was heard and our appellate attorney, Tom Dickinson, took the stand. A timer flashed green, which indicated Tom had ten minutes to present his arguments. Six hundred seconds to plea for freedom.

Jerry and I had watched five preceding cases, civil ones, that were allotted close to forty-five minutes apiece. They were about stocks and bonds, estates, and payroll thievery, none a compelling murder case like Don's. And we have ten minutes?

Tom handled himself well. However, in his allotted time, he could present only Motion One, the issue regarding Judge McHugh's handling of the tape recording. Tom's time was so damn limited. Then, a blinking, yellow warning light flashed, soon to be followed by a red light, and Tom was shut off. He never got a chance to review the Vienna Convention issue of consular rights for a Canadian. I thought TD was direct, well spoken, clear, and appealing to the judges.

On the other hand, Shoshana Stern, the Bristol County assistant district attorney, who represented the prosecution, appeared unsure and unconfident. She talked so softly she could hardly be heard. Shaky, that's what she was.

Vic Blank, who drove to Boston with Tom and attended the hearing, told me he was impressed with the "handsome ambiance" of the courtroom. The room was wood paneled with artwork on the walls. The ceiling about twenty feet high. "The room's capacity is about 200, I think." Vic even wore a suit and tie. Chief Justice Margaret Marshall presided. She occupied most of the ten minutes with questions. Judge Spina, the justice appointed to conduct a preliminary review on behalf of the panel of justices, never said a word. I think he left the room for our case. As mentioned earlier, Spina had recommended denial of Don's two motions.

Prior to the hearing, Bruce Krell told me supreme court justices do their homework. During supreme court sessions, he always watched their body language closely. When I asked TD about this, he indicated he had the MO on all the presiding justices. He had a good feeling about their body language and expects they'll mail him their decision within two months.

April 23, 2008

Some good news. Yesterday, my doctor called giving me a clean bill of health, resulting from a recent colonoscopy (aka a thorough pain in the ass). I've been asked to serve on two boards of directors (my condominium association and the Alaska Writers Guild). I've completed a two-year penalty payment plan to the IRS. I've been catching beautiful rainbow trout. My Red Sox are in first place. And I've got a good vibe about Don's chances.

It's early Tuesday morning. I'm driving along Turnagain Arm on the Seward Highway, my favorite road in the whole wide world. On my way to fish Kenai Lake for rainbows. So thankful, such scenery, nicest day of the year. I'll fish today in comfort; no multi-layers of clothing, no gloves, temperature expected to be in the mid-fifties. Man, am I a lucky guy. Sunny, unclear skies. Unclear because winds are traveling across the Pacific Ocean bringing smoke from forest fires in Russia and sand from severe Mongolian wind storms in the Gobi Desert. I can hardly see mountains in the distance. They look to be fogged in. Can you imagine, the Gobi Desert. That's in central Asia.

My cell phone rings and it's Tom Dickinson. Immediately he says, "I have news. Donald got turned down on his motions."

"Oh no."

"Yes. On Motion Two, the business about the Vienna Convention, they suggested we present it to the superior court. So this was a technical knockout, not a knockout."

"I'm sick."

"I know you are. I didn't want to beat around the bush. Only wish I was delivering better news."

"Me too, Tom. I was hopeful this time around..."

"I'll mail you the paperwork from the Supreme Judicial Court. You might want to go online and read the article in today's *Attleboro Sun Chronicle*. Blodgett's brother is quoted."

"I'll do that."

"I'm sorry, David. When the dust settles I'd like to know what Don's intentions are."

Our conversation ended and I pulled off the side of the road. Just sat there for a while, turned around, and headed home.

The phone rang again. It's Vic Blank. "Have you heard the news?"

"Yes, I just hung up with Tom Dickinson."

"You did?"

"Yes. He told me that Don got turned down by the SJC." There was a long pause. "Vic, are you still there?"

"Yeh. I didn't know that. That's not why I'm calling."

Another long pause. I gulped and held my breath. "Don didn't do anything stupid, did he?"

"No, nothing like that, thank God. However, I just got a letter from him saying that he's spent the last eight days in solitary."

"What?"

"You heard me right — for an attitude adjustment. Seems Don was told that he's being shipped out to the Bridgewater (MA) prison. Not good for a seventy-year-old man, having to pull up stakes from a prison he's adjusted to for so long. Apparently he gave the guards a wrath of shit and they hauled him off to the hole. Gave him a three-inch pencil, no eraser, a few pages of stationery and two envelopes, no stamps. An attitude adjustment the prison officials called it. Can you imagine. Now you're telling me he's been shot down by the SJC?"

"Yes, I am."

"David, I'm gonna hang up now. I'll talk to you soon, OK?"

"OK."

"David?"

"What?"

"One other thing. In Don's last letter he told me your last letter to him was censored. You know they censor letters and apparently some of your context was unsatisfactory as far as they were concerned. Did you send him pornography or something?"

"No, wise guy. But I did send pages of *Deacon's Crossbow* for him to edit."

"Then that must be the problem."

"This is a good day gone bad, Vic."

May 1, 2008

I finally conjured up the nerve to call Ed and Agnes Smith. It galled me to give them bad news. At their age, bad news they don't need.

It wasn't a long conversation. I told Agnes what happened at the supreme court hearing, leaving a ray of hope regarding the consular rights with Canada.

Agnes shared with me an incident that took place on the last day of the trial in New Bedford when Judge McHugh sentenced Don to life without parole.

"I was walking down a corridor about to leave the courtroom. My legs were shaky and I never felt so empty in my life. And who comes walking by me but the judge. What's his name, David?

"Judge McHugh, James McHugh III."

"That's it. I swear the minute I saw him all I could think about was whether he was a Scotsman or not. That name, McHugh, comes from a snobbish Scottish clan. And there he was by my side prancing along. I'll tell you David, it was only my Scottish womanly inhibitions that held me back from telling him a thing or two. But, I didn't and I regret it to this very day."

I did go online and read the *Attleboro Sun Chronicle* article dated April 23, 2008 about the supreme court denial. It pretty much mirrored all the facts that Tom Dickinson shared with me. Below are a few excerpts that I found interesting:

Blodgett's older brother, Ed, praised the SJC's ruling.

"This guy got nothing better to do with his time than to sit there and come up with reasons why he shouldn't be there," Ed Blodgett said.

"He was convicted by the jury. He deserves to be where he is."

Blodgett said Graham's argument about being a Canadian citizen doesn't wash with him.

"His crime was committed in the United States and should be subject to U.S. laws," Blodgett said. "If he can't abide by these rules, he can go back to Canada."

How odd. I think Don would have been pleased if Mr. Blodgett was the judge, because he'd be sent back to Canada.

August 29, 2008

Below are excerpts from the last two letters I received from Don:

Dear Dave,

At the end of this month I was removed forcibly from Souza-Baranowski to Old Colony. I wasn't allowed to bring over $250 of canteen purchases I had in my cell at SBCC. The cells here are smaller and have about 40 square feet of unobstructed floor space. There are no bookshelves like in other prisons and only two coat hangers. Only half my underwear arrived, so I bought more. This week eight other inmates and myself lost our "whites" that were sent to the prison laundry. Next day we lost our "colored" clothing. We finally tracked them down in two separate blocks. I won't bother you with other trivialities. Let me just say, what seems like small potatoes outside is big potatoes inside, to me anyway.

My cellmate is a packrat that doesn't have a dime to spend, so he devotes seventeen hours a day mooching off me. He's a pacer, in the cell, and there ain't too much room to pace! He had the cell to himself for five months, and now, I suspect, feels crowded. I feel the same way. He's not a bad guy except he misses the toilet at night. I don't go barefoot in the dark anymore; keep my shower shoes handy. Trying to teach him to sit and pee, but he's in his 70s and early Alzheimer's is setting in, so he prefers to stand and spray.

These cells were designed for single occupancy back in the 80s. We have 125 men in a common room with seating for less than thirty. Most of the 125 use English as a second language.

Several letters to write. Will write again soon.

Take care.

Don

October 7, 2008

I awoke this morning from a blurry nightmare. I know it involved the Grahams as well as Blodgett and Robert Astin. The setting was right there, out on Route 95, at the scene of the incident. It was mostly about Astin, because somehow Donald assigned me to keep an eye on Astin, and, for the life of me, I couldn't find him, which made the dream all the more anxsty. Finally, I spotted Astin standing on the side of the road. He was as frightened as I was, on a mission he had no taste for. I tried to talk to him but he soon just evaporated into midair.

I wonder if he has nightmares. Truth is, I've tried to contact Mr. Astin, by phone and through the mail. He's either ignored my correspondence or never got the messages. Regardless, I feel for him. No one should have to experience such an unnecessary tragedy.

If I ever got a chance to meet him, I'd like to ask the following questions:
Does the incident haunt you?
Has it changed your life?
Are you still an EMT?
Where were you going on that fateful night?
Any comments you want to make about Mr. Blodgett, his personality, temperament, his feelings?
Did you know that Blodgett had problems with the law?
Did you consider him a top-notch EMT?
Because he was older than you, did you look up to him?
Regarding friendship, on a scale of 1 to 10, 1 being no friend and 10 being like a brother, what would you rate your friendship with Mr. Blodgett?
Do you stay in touch with any of Mr. Blodgett's family?
What were you guys talking about before stopping?
Exactly why did Blodgett stop?
Why did you both get out of the car?
Why did Graham take chase in the first place? And why do you suppose Graham pulled in behind you?
When Graham got out of his car, did he strike you as dangerous?
Once out of the car, you indicated Graham never gave a warning. Were any words exchanged at all?

What went through your mind when Blodgett got hit?

Did you attend the whole trial?

What was it like when you first saw Graham at the trial?

Are there any additional facts of interest you can share that were not taken up in the trial, or after the trial?

Is there anything you want to tell me that I haven't asked?

Do you feel sorry for Graham at all?

Fourteen years later, do you think Donald Graham should still be in the can?

Robert Astin does know all.

He was there.

Chapter Ten

Home and Home

December 4, 2008

I came. I saw. I condensed.

Left Anchorage on November 24 for Rhode Island and returned this morning at 0200, exhausted. I condensed a year into ten days.

On Thanksgiving morning I drove through Woonsocket, past an empty Barry Field because the Cumberland vs Woonsocket football game was at Cumberland High this year. Stopped at *Because He Lives,* which was packed with poor folks enjoying a Thanksgiving brunch, and said hello to Pat Dempster, who is still the director of *Because He Lives.* Pat was in good spirits, she looked good. She was pleased to hear that I'd be visiting Don. "Tell Donald I pray for Sandra and him."

Woonsocket, my dear old home town, now reminds me of a comedian who no longer gets laughs. The city seems to have withered. *The Providence Journal* reports that Rhode Island's unemployment rate is 9.3 percent and it's always higher in Woonsocket. The hard part for me was getting back that old spirit and vibrancy during the years of my residency.

I continued on to the cemetery that domiciles my parents, to say hello and hopefully gain some spiritual at-oneness. For the second consecutive year, the gates were locked, so all I could do was stand on the sidewalk and glance through the iron fence, looking for their gravesites. I hoped I'd feel something, something spiritual, but I just felt bad that I couldn't get in.

We had the best Thanksgiving dinner ever. Our Bellwing Farm turkey was brown and juicy. Grandson Cole is now bigger than the turkey. The Reisling wine fit. Everyone was in good spirits.

Throughout the week I visited with friends, shopped, enjoyed live music in Newport, and even fished the Providence River. On Saturday evening we all ventured over to the Mount St. Charles rink to watch my son Luke play in an alumni hockey game. Hockey at The Mount, just those words give me a rush. Luke surprised us by scoring two goals. It's still freezing in that damn rink.

I spent considerable time with Cole, now fifteen months old, plump and perfect. He's got big blue eyes and never stops smiling and laughing. The kid looks at me with suspicion, maybe sensing I'm 66 years his senior and we don't have much in common. Soon, he'll be walking and gramps will be wobbling.

On the Monday after Thanksgiving I drove up to the Old Colony Correctional Center from North Smithfield, Rhode Island to Bridgewater, Massachusetts. About an hour's drive. Unfortunately, Vic Blank could not join me. The OCCC is a large complex of old prison buildings and a hospital. Took me a while to find Donald's building. The rules and regs for visitors are the same as the SBCC. OCCC is a medium-security prison.

In short order I was seated with Don, who was wearing jeans and a sweatshirt. He looked OK, not as good as the times I visited him at the SBCC. I think life with a demented cellmate is taking it's toll, especially with the two of them being confined in a 5-by-8-foot cell. Don told me, "Back at the SBCC, when they came to deliver me here, I refused to go. So they shackled me and dragged me to the hole, where I stayed for eight days. Then they beat me out of canteen money."

I didn't ask Don who "they" were. Most of our chat was mundane, flat with nothing out of the ordinary to report. Action is suspended as we wait for Jeff Pine to take over from Tom Dickinson. I felt like shit being in a prison again, wishing by now Don would be on the outside. How he sustains is beyond me, his adaptability amazes me. I left after an hour, upset with myself that I could not be a more refreshing visitor.

The following evening I had dinner with Vic Blank. It was like being at Floru's Restaurant in Woonsocket in the good old days, except we were at Chelo's Restaurant in North Providence. Floru's no longer exists.

"Ten years ago we'd have a martini. Now we order tea."

"Are you OK?" I asked.

"About a 4.2. All because of you."

"Me? What the hell did I do?"

Pointing his finger in my direction, he said, "You're the one who got me involved in this madness. When we were younger, we'd talk about the stock market, our kids, business problems, movies, women, baseball. Now all we talk about is Donald Graham."

"I'm sorry."

"Don't be." He lowered his finger. "You know I'm kidding." Vic paused, which he often does these days, talking slower, more deliberately. "Truth be known, I'm thankful to you. Having this cause is very special. I've often wondered, especially since retirement, if I'd ever have another cause in my lifetime. That's a little scary, you know. Not having any pots-of-gold-at-the-end-of-the-rainbow kind of thing, other than the Grim Reaper waiting out in the fields." He nodded. "But Don is a cause. A cause of consequence. Donald Graham's cause and circumstance is like no other I've ever had. Now, he's become a new friend. We have so much in common; Don's a bridge player, a Civil War buff, we both root for the New England Patriots, he reads the same books. For me, he's therapy. I have a pen pal at age seventy-seven."

"Maybe you should move in at the Old Colony Correctional Center?"

Vic smiled, then soberly said, "That's why I'm a 4.2. Donald S. Graham should be having dinner with us right now. Instead he's a life-without-paroler. All because of road rage, which in some medical circles they now call *intermittent explosive disorder* (IED).

"Whatever they call it, it ain't good."

"Recently I read an article by the chairman of psychology at the University of Chicago. He's actually studying road rage. He claims that this bad behavior involves inadequate production of serotin, a mood regulating brain chemical. So, road rage has gone biological.

"Maybe, in time, this study could alter Don's sentence?"

Vic frowned. "I don't know. Maybe."

"Speaking of studies, did you know that in the state of California, if you get certain traffic violations you're required to attend Traffic School?"

"That's the case for most states."

"Right. My buddy Dan Moreno was telling me he has a friend who was forced to attend. As part of the class, road rage was addressed, and guess who was featured?"

"You gotta be kidding me?"

"Nope. All about Donald. I think they even included his interview with Dan Rather. The moral to the story story – Don't let what happened to Don happen to you."

"My God, Don's a celebrity."

"In California anyway. Maybe other states present the same program." I groaned and opened the palms of my hands in dismay. "At times it all seems unreal, huh. I bet I've shared Don's story with over fifty people. All of them expressed sadness and remorse. Not hatred, but remorse. That reaction says *life without parole* is the wrong sentence. Therein lies the core difference between Don and a hardened, ruthless criminal. The ruthless deserve *life without*. Don deserves a lesser sentence."

"That's an interesting slant," Vic replied.

"But it's true. Ya know, for the life of me, I'll never understand why Sandra Graham wasn't a more convincing witness. Seems to me, having solid credentials, like being the secretary to a high school principal, her testimony should have been most convincing. She could have won the day. I question how well Don's lawyers, Lutes and Cooper, counseled her. Didn't Sandra see Blodgett carrying the flashlight? Didn't Sandra hear Don give verbal warning? If I had been in her shoes, I'd be screaming my head off at Astin in that courtroom, calling him a liar, standing up in defense of my husband. It just doesn't make sense to me."

"I'm afraid it doesn't."

"On the other hand I can't help but sympathize with Sandra's family, the Thibault's from Cape Cod. Imagine how they feel. Their incarcerated son-in-law, a lifer. And they have to deal with that on a daily basis."

"Like going from high water to hell."

"No kidding. Their social life must be severely limited. Folks must look at them and whisper, 'They're related to the road rage guy.'" I paused, as though not wanting to conjure up what I was about to say. "Then Sandra died. Can you believe it?"

"Beyond imagination."

"My heart breaks for that family."

"I think it's called collateral damage." Vic looked away.

For sanity sake I changed the conversation. "And then there's Robert Astin's testimony. He actually claimed that Don never gave warning. Please. Donald was deacon of his church. Deacons are deacons because they're talkers. He testified under oath that he did, and I believe him. Why didn't the jury believe Donald? Everything Robert Astin said was accepted as gospel. Like he was a choir boy. No debris was thrown at the Grahams. Astin had no recall of Blodgett carrying a flashlight. Making Deacon Don a total liar in the eyes of judge and jury. And they bought into it. I don't get it."

"I don't get it either." Vic opened the palms of his hands. "Maybe Don didn't give warning."

"Maybe he was so unnerved, he thought he shouted out, but in reality he didn't. Maybe, but I don't think so," I said, and hesitated. "Then again, on the flip, Don's father was a hunter, and Don himself was a soldier. Hunters and soldiers don't give their position away." I paused. "Ya know, it really doesn't matter. The side of the road was well lit by street lamps and Blodgett was holding a flashlight illuminating the entire scene. I'm certain it was pointed directly into Don's eyes. Had to be. That's why the guy had the flashlight, a weapon of convenience. That crossbow had to appear as clear as a burning road flare. Ya know, Don's lawyer should have shined a flashlight into the eyes of each jury member."

"And where the hell is that flashlight?"

"I don't know." I became more animated and fired up. "Even if... Wait, let's accept all of Astin's testimony. One thing Astin owned up to is that Blodgett pulled off the road ahead of Graham. Blodgett and Astin stopped first. That's an action, not a reaction. Doesn't matter if they were stopping to help Graham out or to beat the shit out of him. They stopped first.

"Graham reacted by pulling in. Then, Blodgett and Astin got out of their car. That's an action." I paused. "They advanced. That's an aggressive action in anyone's book. Astin testified that Blodgett said to Graham, 'What the hell do you think you're doing?' Tough words. It wasn't like saying, 'Can we help you out? We're EMTs and thought you were in distress.'"

"Not exactly Avon calling."

"Hell no. When Blodgett pulled over and stopped, that action alone commenced the final act of the incident. Blodgett had the ball; first and ten. Every move Graham made was a reaction. That dictates self-defense, not first-degree murder. It also differentiates the definitions of road rage and self-defense, don't you think?"

"I couldn't agree more," Vic replied.

"The truth is, every action Don took that night is contrary to premeditation of an *atrocious* act, if you ask me. How can you equate premeditated murder with a guy who just got done with round dance lessons? I mean, come on, this sounds like the makings of a scene from *The Sound of Music*. Then when those guys stopped in the middle of Route 95 and Don slipped into adrenaline overload, that's not malice aforethought. He had trouble controlling the shakes for Chrise sakes. That's not how a hardened criminal operates. Not, I say."

"You're right."

"I think I am. I don't know. I feel like we're at the Last Supper or something."

Vic nodded. "Don's counsel had to be comatose. We could review countless road rage cases and I bet less than 10 percent get life without."

"But in Massachusetts…" We both shrugged. I opened my hands and said, "We should change the subject."

"Impossible."

"Try."

"I spoke to Ed Baram this morning," Vic said.

"How is Eddie?"

"The same. Told me to tell you that he thinks about Donald Graham."

"That is not changing the subject."

"Like I said, it's impossible," Vic replied. "When Eddie volunteered in the kitchen at *Because He Lives* — this was several years after Don's incarceration — Ed said the old-timers always talked about Don. The words were good. Everyone liked him.

"Regarding the tragedy itself, Eddie said Don did something he wouldn't dare do. Wouldn't have the guts. Ed has nothing but admiration for the guy. He said, 'I would have run or taken the beating.'"

"Ya know, Vic, at the point of no return, not many people could pull that trigger. I'm tellin' ya, killing someone is nuts, hard to do, knowing it will stay with you till the big confession."

"Since we last talked about pulling the trigger, I've given that possibility plenty of thought, and, ya know what? You're right, I couldn't do it."

"Of course you couldn't," I acknowledged. "Then again, maybe, just maybe, there's a one-half of one percent chance in you that could lock, load, and squeeze. It's scary shit. It's a world beyond us, Vic. We don't know about weapons, firearms, never mind crossbows. We've never gone out to the woods to shoot. By our very nature, we don't think about life and death confrontations."

"But those that do…"

"And ask questions later." I nodded. "They can kill."

Vic said, "Donald Graham had the option to shoot earlier on, but he did not. He could have shot both those guys in the back, for crying out loud, which might have qualified him for an atrocious first-degree murder charge, but he didn't do that."

"No he didn't. That's a hell of a point. One his counsel should have brought up. Don actually made a less aggressive move by retreating from the back of his car."

Vic glanced across the room. "I'm too passive." He then gave me a sad look. "I'm incapable of hurting anyone, never mind killing. Maybe I'm a coward."

"I wouldn't lose sleep over that one," I reassured him. "Listen, I'll tell ya something else I dwell on. Think about it, out of this whole mess only one person gained."

"What do you mean?" Vic asked.

"Assistant District Attorney John Letourneau. It was a loss for everyone else, a tragedy. But for Letourneau, he gained that all-important notch on his first-degree-verdict belt. This is the only person in the whole lot who gained from this verdict."

"Interesting point."

"Yes it is. I've often wondered about Letourneau and Judge McHugh, these men of plaintive ways. I wonder if they have children … a daughter say. What would happen if either one of them were driving down the road and spotted some jackass dangerously tailgating a young schoolgirl? Would these deacons of justice keep driving and ignore such behavior?

"Imagine either of them getting into such a fix. Put Letourneau or McHugh in Graham's shoes. What would they say if they took action against the likes of Michael Blodgett? 'I'm sorry, I lost my head. Slap my hand. I should have let them beat the shit out of my wife and me.' Or would they say, 'I'm a proud and worthy man. I love my wife, my family, I believe in right versus wrong, and I could not ignore what I saw on the road. No sir, I stand up for my rights. I pulled over. I pulled the trigger. Now give me a medal for courage.'"

"Don Graham gets life without parole," Vic replied.

"And John Letourneau gets a notch on his belt."

"Fait accompli."

I pointed my finger at Vic. "Talk about an unlevel playing field, Judge McHugh did allow the prosecution to display all five of Don's crossbows in clear view of the jury." I lowered my finger saying, "If I were Don's counsel, I would have vehemently objected to those five weapons of lethal destruction."

"I totally agree," Vic nodded. "What do you have there?"

I held up a newspaper article. "This comes from *The Woonsocket Call* and is dated August 11, 1997, written by Russ Olivo, the staff writer who covered the case.

"Listen to this. 'Assistant District Attorney John Letourneau, the prosecutor in the case, said the Massachusetts Supreme Judicial Court will no doubt modify the life-with-no-possibility-of-parole sentence if there are grounds for it. The high court could even grant him a new trial.'"

"Wow."

"Wow is right. *No doubt,* those were Letourneau's very words. Words coming from the prosecutor himself."

Vic shook his head. "It's scary because we lost our supreme court attempt for retrial this past April." He paused. "But they left a door open, suggesting Donald go back to the superior court on the Canada thing, meaning the fat lady hasn't sung yet."

"Maybe John Letourneau knows the answer? Maybe he'd be willing to help us out now that fourteen years have passed?"

"Wouldn't that be something. It would be like a fox returning eggs to the chicken coop."

Then Vic asked, "David, could you pull that crossbow trigger?"

"No." I quickly answered, then reconsidered. "Hold on. I don't know."

"Not good enough. I want a yes-or-no answer."

"It's circumstantial."

"Yes or no?"

"It's circumstantial. If my back was to the wall. If my wife or children were endangered..."

"Yes?"

"I'd pull the fucking trigger."

"You're one-hundred percent certain of that?"

"Ninety-nine point three percent."

"This whole thing is just awful."

"It sure is," I replied. "Last week Maureen and I were talking about Don's options, and she says to me, 'This thing never would have happened if your buddy had a cell phone. He could have dialed up 911, reported it, and been on his way.'"

So, I'm back in Alaska after my visit to Rhode Island. Spent quality time with family and friends. Spent gobs of time in airports during the two dreary journeys totaling twenty-one hours in the air and covering some 11,000 miles. To go home, then turn around and go home.

I just remembered something Donald said during my visit to the Old Colony pen. "The bolt entered Blodgett's shoulder sideways." I remember he emphatically pointed at a slant toward my shoulder. "Had it gone in straight, it would have missed the artery! Can you imagine, I'm a quarter inch from being a free man."

That prison visit was uncomfortable. The visiting room was uncomfortable; knowing Don's cell was uncomfortable made me uncomfortable. Knowing when we were done, after Don's shakedown, he'd be returning to a 5-by-8-foot cell built for dwarfs, with a demented cell mate waiting for him, made me uncomfortable. The hardened fact that Don was still incarcerated made everything uncomfortable.

December 15, 2008

Every time I dial up Ed and Agnes Smith I feel like I'm calling family, stepping into their Moncton, New Brunswick existence of simple love, dignity, and prayer. We last talked back in May. It was not a happy call, because lawyer Dickinson had just lost his appeal with the Massachusetts Supreme Court.

Ed answered and told me, "I must turn you over to Agnes because she hears better." And then I heard Agnes' sweet voice. "I've been thinking about you, David. Now I can listen to you."

"Agnes, I have better news since our last conversation."

"Just hearing your voice makes it a better day."

"I feel the same way, Agnes, every time we speak. It's a curious thing that we've become so close, from so far away, because of your nephew and my friend."

"It's true. Ed and I give thanks that you're trying so hard for Donnie."

"Appreciate that, Agnes. You know we can be thankful for Vic Blank's help too."

"Oh yes. We know all about Mr. Blank. Donald has spoken very highly of him."

"Good. I'm pleased to hear that." I paused with hopes of gaining her full attention. At ninety years old, I figure that can be hard to do at times. "Agnes, listen carefully…" I did my best to explain that former Rhode Island Attorney General Jeffrey Pine would be taking over Don's case.

"You know David, it's been fourteen years, a long time filled with pain and sorrow, and as God is my witness, it's taken its toll. I only hope destiny is short-lived. We miss Donnie." Her sigh and pain filtered through the phone from five thousand miles away. "So, we continue to hope and pray." She paused, purposely changing the subject. "By the way, how are you doing with the book?"

"That's the other reason I'm calling. I've written an ending. I was hoping it would be a happy one, a celebration. I waited and waited. I couldn't take forever, so I brought it to a conclusion." I pictured Agnes sitting there in an old, sturdy, wooden chair with an oak table by her side where she keeps the phonebook; she's attentive to my words and Ed is by her side picking up on prompts. A Norman Rockwell painting.

"I'm sure you've given it plenty of thought, David."

"Yes I have. I'd like to mail you about ten pages for your approval, if that's OK."

"Go right ahead."

"There are some personal pages and I just wanted to make sure I didn't miss anything."

"You feel free to send them on, David."

"Thanks again, Agnes. You've become like a mother and a sister to me. I swear to God."

"Oh my, what a lovely compliment. I'm blushing." She paused. "But, you know David, most people only see my good side. I can be very difficult in close quarters. I understand the dark side of things. There's some in everyone, isn't there?"

"I suppose there is, Agnes."

"What was your mother like, David?"

The question took me by surprise; took me a few seconds to deliver an answer. "You would have loved her. I see you both as two peas in the same pod. She was part philosopher and psychiatrist, terrific cook, a mixer. Dolly Brown loved to have a good time."

"Tell me more."

"Let's see. Well, she was a fair person. I remember on my first day of junior high school, I came home and told her I saw a nigger. 'What?' she asked. She was startled, eyes almost popping out of her head. By the way, both Dolly and I have large eyes."

"You called your mother Dolly?"

"I did. She was just like a sister, like one of the gang, so much fun to have around that I'd actually take her along on dates when I was a high schooler. Swear to God. Everyone had such a good time. My date would like me more, just because of Dolly."

"I can just picture her."

"So, back to junior high school. She sits me down, Agnes. Remember it so well, it seems like yesterday. Whenever she told me to sit down, I knew it was serious stuff. And she tells me to never, never, for the rest of my life, judge a person by the color of their skin. 'That's a very bad thing, as you will come to understand. Take each person one at a time and judge them by their moral character.' She told me that in 1954 and I've heeded those words ever since."

"I wish I knew her."

"She's been gone since 1991. I know you'd have hit it off. Tell ya something strange though, Agnes." I hesitated, momentarily not sure if I should reveal what I was about to say. "My mother was a verbal abuser. Wicked, I'm tellin' ya. During my high school years she never missed a dinner when she didn't tear into me. Now, looking back, it didn't exactly help my self-esteem."

"Oh, that's very sensitive information, David. But, I confess I believe you and somehow understand." She pondered her next words. "Don't be too hard on your mother. There are reasons for everything." She drew a breath. "You know, it was not so easy for Donnie with his father and all. It's a paradox. And *that's* why I think Donnie became so caring. *That's* why he's in jail, because he worried so much for the girl Michael Blodgett was following on that terrible night." Agnes paused. "Instead of minding his own business. He's always been that way, quiet and caring."

"Strange fate."

"And then he learned about bitterness."

"Bitterness?"

"Yes, bitterness. I first heard it when Donnie and his father returned from their summer in the bush, way up there in Quebec. This was between Donnie's freshman and sophomore years in college at the University of New Brunswick.

So when they got back that time, they stayed at our house. That first night Frank did something displeasing to Donnie, and he shouts, 'Shut up, Dad.' Believe me, I was stunned. Had never in all my life heard such harshness come out of that boy's mouth. Knowing that Frank was no angel, I still told Donnie, 'This is no way to talk to your father.' Frank stood up and threw a chair in his son's direction and left the house. Donnie lowered his head into his hands and wept.

"We adored that boy so much, and to see him so hurt and humbled, why...," Agnes sighed, "it tore my heart apart. Usually he was quiet, just like his father. That side of the family, the Grahams, were a quiet lot. Lots of silence, short sentences, nodding gestures.

"As soon as Frank left, Donnie said to me, 'I have more morals in my little toe than my father has in his entire body.' I'll never forget those words. They've stayed with me like the mark of Cain. All I could surmise is that boy saw too much of the dark side during that summer in the bush."

"Ya know, Agnes, up here in Alaska I've met several sour characters. They're called sourdoughs as a matter of fact. Life in the bush is claustrophobic. It can twist the mind."

"I suppose you're right. Here's something else, and David, I've never shared this with anyone. It's something my sister Elva told me, Donnie's mother, may her soul rest in peace. Little Donnie was only three months old, so let's see, that would be 1939. Late one night Elva heard strange and loud noises. So loud it woke up baby Donnie. Elva took him from the crib and walked to the window.

"Out by the barn, Frank's father, Austin Graham, was whipping a two-horse team attached to a wagon. Grandpa snapped that whip so hard, it cut deep slashes in the hide of them poor creatures. Whippin' em so bad, the horse's screams and his whoops echoed in the trees. Elva told me she could see terror in the eyes of those horses. She could never understand how a man could be so cruel. And, I'll never forget her words either. Said with such ernest. It makes me cringe and wonder what creates such a distorted disposition. How a man could let misspent power become bigger than him."

"My God, Agnes."

"I know. One generation misguiding the next. But David, may God be my judge, Donnie was the opposite of his granddaddy and father. He was not very interested in hunting or fishing. Archery, yes. He understood all about takin' down a critter, dressing and filleting, but kept at arms length. I remember when he was about thirteen when my husband, who Donald respected immensely, ordered Donnie to cut up some liver. Poor boy performed the chore, but we could see he was so uncomfortable that Ed had him stop."

"He wasn't a hardcore like most hunters and woodsmen?"

"That's right, David."

"I'll be damned. That means when he shot Blodgett he must have been beside himself."

"He may not have showed it on the surface; but, I'm sure you are right. I remember when he called me from Rhode Island the day after the incident. He was beside himself. He kept repeating, 'But you don't understand Auntie, I shot a man. I killed him.'"

"How awful."

"And during the eight-day trial, even after his sentencing, and then in prison, he has always portrayed himself as bitter and heartless, when I know deep down where his true spiritual soul lay. He's heartbroken, even for the likes of Michael Blodgett."

Sleep was impossible last night. Truth is, I couldn't stop thinking about Grampa Austin Graham whipping those poor horses. Even if he was in a drunken stupor, what the hell was he doing? What did a three-month old Donald see and feel? What transcended from mother to child as she held him by the window? What lasting effect did it have on all of them? I just kept running possibilities through my mind, like, what was Gramp's frame of mind when he woke up the next morning?

No, this would not be a night of much sleep. My attention shifted to Donald's father. I wanted him to materialize, to appear from out of the past, from hell or from heaven or purgatory, from wherever his soul remains, so I could know him, know what made him tick.

My mind became graphic and I envisioned three brainscans in front of one of those bright x ray lights you see in a medical office; one each of grandfather, father and son, all filled with wavy, complex lines spaced below descriptive words of character like good and evil. And I tried to weave these three relationships to the tragedy of February 20, 1994.

I worked these thoughts and images through the night until I resigned myself into thinking I was at a helpless standstill. That there was so much missing in my quantum message that everything I've reported in this project contains scant meaning; no lesson, no value, no consequence. The last thing I remember before falling asleep was the realization that men have proven, time and time again, to be inept leaders, and that Agnes should become President of the World.

The following day I conjured up new wrinkles based on Agnes becoming President of the World. I made a circle and placed the following people around it. Donald's grandfather, his father, Donald himself, Michael Blodgett, Assistant District Attorney John Letourneau, Judge James McHugh III. I even included Robert Astin. And me. In the middle I placed Agnes. Poor Agnes, surrounded by men. Like a bolt of clarity, it occurred to me that all of us are at war. And that's what this world of ours is about, what we've been doing *ad infinitum*. Destroying, hating, and killing each other.

Donald's tragic incident took on a lesser role in the whole scheme of things, which for three-and-a-half years seemed impossible, because I've been eating, drinking, and sleeping Donald Graham's plight. But for me to see the greater light, I needed to reduce his tragedy to better see the truth. The true picture evolved out of my circle. One that told me men must put down their swords, once and for all. If Donald Graham and Michael Blodgett had been void of testosteronic evil and hatred, as it could have been for a horse-whipping grandfather and an insensitive father, the tragedy of February 20, 1994 would not have occurred.

Maybe it's too late given the conditions of our world. I don't know. I do know that Donald Graham's crime <u>does not</u> warrant first degree murder / life without parole. I'll take that to my grave. However, today Donald's persona changed for me. It has nothing to do with liking or not liking him. Instead, it has to do with pride and ignorance and lack of respect, macho stupidity and insensitivity. What men have been bred to do throughout the ages.

And it was sweet Agnes, with her infinite wisdom, who brought this to light. A loyal aunt who adores her Donnie, but deep down possesses basic motherly instinct and a true understanding of right versus wrong. She understands that generational acts displayed from a possessed grandfather, to a father who lost the respect of his son, to the son himself, merged their mentalities to create the macabre outcome on the chilling night of February 20, 1994; when, with vengeance and malice, Michael Blodgett walked his last walk and Donald Graham fired his deadly weapon.

In a way it embarrasses me to be a man. That all of those careless people in the circle are men. That men go to war. That women fight, but do not go to war. And that's true you know, if for the simple reason that they bear, they procreate. A woman thinks from her heart and her heart dictates to her intelligence.

What I've come to understand from this whole affair is that men, in order to lead, must learn womanly intuitions, or we are doomed. Since boys grew muscles and the first arrow was drawn, men have led this forlorn world. Therefore, if there truly is a moral to this tragic story, it's time for men to put their childish ways aside. Agnes knows. And now Donnie does too.

It's winter again, mid-December, 2010. Two years since that last conversation with Agnes.

So fast the seasons come and go, they just blend into each other like mixed oil paint on an artist's palette. Back in New England several harbingers of winter's coldness lurk inexorably to bitter Januaries and Februaries. Here in Alaska, temperatures plummet south into negative digits and most everything is snow-covered. Constants, like a lifer's time spent behind bars.

Former Rhode Island Attorney General Jeff Pine has spent time in the employ of Donald. Our hopes were high when Jeff took over the case. He started by preparing a costly "overview" of all legal action(s) going back to day one. Vic Blank and I questioned the necessity of this because we already know everything that's happened from day one. However, this is what Jeff did. We hope it has functional purpose.

Pine also prepared and presented a package to Massachusetts Governor Deval Patrick. His objective was to have the governor commute Donald's sentence, which in layman's terms is similar to asking for a pardon. When I heard of this strategy, I had visions of Jeff using his political power as a former Rhode Island attorney general to gain personal entry into Governor Duval's confidence. I picture Jeff knocking on the governor's door, introducing himself, and saying, "I've come regarding a client of mine who I believe deserves commutation. How about a cup of coffee, Governor?"

As part of the commutation package, Jeff asked me to prepare a letter on Donald's behalf. One of testimony, a personal message expressing what I know about Don. I immediately agreed.

Here is my letter:

November 4, 2008

Dear Governor Deval Patrick,

My name is David G. Brown and I've been a resident of Anchorage, Alaska since 2004. I spent most of my life in Woonsocket, Rhode Island from birth through high school. In the early 60s I attended college at Suffolk University in Boston, followed by a tour in the

Naval Reserve from 1963 to 1969, then back to Woonsocket as an insurance executive. I have two grown sons and two former wives. I was active on several boards of directors. Politically, I'm an Independent. I've always adored sports and have played many. Presently, I'm a fishing addict and Alaska has become my dream come true. In 1997 I sold my business and returned to college to study my favorite discipline, creative writing. That's pretty much what I do these days, fish and write, as well as spend time with my partner, Maureen, and our beloved Australian terrier, Kaya.

I know Donald S. Graham very well. I want you to know that the following words of testimony on his behalf are fair, sincere and heartfelt.

Mr. Graham is a longtime friend and client dating back to the 1980s and is presently serving a first-degree-murder / life-without-parole sentence effective November of 1995 for an incident that occurred on 2/20/94. This highly publicized road rage incident of international dimensions was god-awful, resulting in the death of Michael David Blodgett from Attleboro, Massachusetts. I do not condone Graham's action(s). I do know, at the moment of no return, he was fearful for both his and his wife's lives. It is the opinion of virtually everyone I know, who is familiar with the case, that *life without* was an incorrect sentence. It's now fifteen years later and Donald Graham remains incarcerated at the Old Colony prison.

Governor Patrick, allow me to present to you the Don Graham I know:

He was a deacon of the First Baptist Church of Woonsocket and I was their insurance agent. He handled all business issues for the church and we met twice a year to review the policies. As time passed we developed a friendship along with our business relationship. I took to liking Don because of his dry wit and straightforward convictions. His honesty. He was and is a man of vision. For example, with the help of several caring people in the Woonsocket community, Don founded the *Because He Lives* mission, a soup kitchen located in the basement of the Church. I handled their insurance needs, and am pleased that *Because He Lives* still exists, serving hundreds of Woonsocket's needy. Don's vision.

Earlier on, he built a distinguished military career earning the right to serve in the renowned 101st Airborne Division, immortalized by author Stephen Ambrose. He served during the Cuban missile crisis of JFK's presidency. Oddly, Don never relinquished his Canadian citizenship, which he maintains to this day. Post army, he opened a floor-cleaning business and eventually gained employment at the General Motors plant in Framingham, from which he retired with pension.

Going further back in time, Graham lived at the home of his aunt and uncle, Ed and Agnes Smith of Fredericton, New Brunswick. He moved in with the Smiths at age ten after his mother passed away. Fortunately, the Smith's were solid taskmasters as well as loving step parents. I've had lengthy conversations with the Smiths, especially Agnes, a former English teacher. Their stories are always laced with love and admiration for their "Donnie." I know they grieve on a daily basis. Things that stand out during Don's Canadian residency include his working at different jobs during high school, playing varsity basketball, acting in school plays, and earning good grades. He was also a member of a contract bridge foursome that included his high school principal, Colin Barrett, who, based on conversations, holds admiration and respect for Donald to this day. Donald was valedictorian of his graduating class.

I spent quality time with Don and got to know his wife and three sons. They married in the early 60s just as Don joined the army, and later settled into a one-family frame dwelling in Woonsocket. Their home was filled with interesting treasures from humorous stories to a harpoon framed on the living room wall. A busy place. Sandra was secretary to the Woonsocket high school principal and a Deacon at the First Baptist Church of Woonsocket, as well as the secretary of their round dance organization. Both Don and Sandra were avid round dancers. They raised gorgeous Himalayan cats. And Don, unlike his father who was considered one of New Brunswick's finest deer hunters, was an excellent bow and arrow target shooter. I always felt safe in the Graham home. He is of Scottish extraction with a family history of soldiering embroidered in the Graham legacy.

As you can tell, Don Graham's story is not all roses and daffodils. He comes from a life of hardship, losing his mother at a young age, having a father who was constantly on the road, and having to work and pay for a college education. There was a bout with alcoholism that was remedied in the 70s with the help of AA. His wife, Sandra, died prematurely. Donald was allowed to attend the funeral and was summarily returned to prison. In prison he meditates, prays, constantly reads, and exercises daily. He has formed bridge groups and cribbage tournaments and actively participates in the prison's AA program.

I have photographs, several of them, which I'm looking at now. If they were enclosed you'd see "Donnie" as a child, standing next to a cousin, wearing a sailor's outfit and a lovable smile. Next, he's sitting in his father's lap along with mom. Another, with two cousins, he stands beside them full of youthful verve, square-jawed, and wearing a tie. And yet another, as a young teenager in knickers with family members. All happy, loving pics taken in New Brunswick. I have photos from his high school graduation, during his military career, and while he was on trial. Many of them break my heart.

During the last five years, because of my obsession to one day see my friend set free, I've written a book entitled *Deacon's Crossbow*, which is presently in the hands of a literary agent.

Governor Patrick, now you know that Donald's contributions to society far outweigh his one moment of regrettable indiscretion. He has paid dearly with fifteen years of hard time. I fervently hope you see fit to commute his sentence. If you do, I am certain he will conduct the remainder of his life as a model citizen.

Thanking you in advance for your compassionate consideration.

Sincerely,

David G. Brown

Sister Darlene and Donald (1944)

Darlene and Donald (1952)

January 11, 2011

I took my annual pilgrimage back to Rhode Island for Thanksgiving week.

On Friday, November 26 I picked up Vic Blank at his home in Cumberland and we headed up to the Souza-Baranowski prison, where Don has been re-transferred, only this time to the Medium Security Section. This seemingly endless series of transfers almost legitimizes the expression, "everything that goes around, comes around." Always thought this was a cockeyed way to look at things; however, when I review the timetable of Don Graham's incarceration from November 1995 to today's date, I'm thinking the adage may have some credibility.

Vic and I went through the sign-in process like old pros and took our seat in the waiting area. After an hour a guard appeared and told us there were problems in the prison and no visitors would be allowed entry until the problem was solved. "No telling how long this will take," he advised. "Chances are no one will be admitted till tomorrow." We waited another two hours and called it quits.

After months of procrastination, this past summer attorney Jeff Pine's commutation package was submitted to a review board that studies commutation requests sent to Governor Patrick. They, in turn, submit it to the governor. I suspect all the requests do not reach the governor's desk. A harrowing thought. To date and most importantly, nary a word from Governor Patrick.

To stoke a flame of discontent Don has lost confidence in his attorney and terminated his services. Jeff Pine has been replaced by a New Bedford lawyer, Greta Janusz. I immediately wrote Don asking his permission to contact Attorney Janusz to offer any assistance I could give.

Don wrote back the following letter of which I've included excerpts:

Dear David,

The freeze-up during your visit happened in my block when an inmate from another block gave some canteen items to an inmate in my block, a no-no, and the block officer took it away from him. Bad inmate! The officer took the "contraband" canteen items up to the podium (his workstation) with the inmate in hot pursuit — no major casualties. This was the orientation unit for incoming prisoners, none of whom are allowed to bring any canteen from their prior location — coffee/food items are at a premium under these conditions. That's the reason Vic and you could not gain admission. What can I say?

I don't know why Jeff did not want to do a Rule 30 after he had finished my request for commutation. [Translated, this means Don wanted Jeff to ask for a new trial because his Constitutional Rights were violated when Judge McHugh conducted the first day of jury selection behind closed doors, when it's supposed to be conducted in public.] Perhaps his heart was just not into it because he spent so many years on the prosecutorial side of the law. Who knows?

I recently found out from other inmates that Greta has a habit of taking three or four years to finish a case and so I wrote her a week ago to stop working on my case and return my day-one trial transcript. She had obtained a CD disc of my entire trial transcript and was going to review that looking for other issues. I wrote her that Jeff already did that and sent her a copy of his analysis, but she persisted on this path.

That's when I was clued in to the fact that her practice consisted of writing letters to inmates — ¼ hour per — and easy legal fee money for her. I was given the name of a go-getter lawyer, Patricia Quintilian, and wrote her earlier today.

Shirley Medium has six housing units, A-D, each unit containing two separate blocks of 60 cells. You have to go outside to go to any of the programs — AA, church, medical, dining hall, property, canteen, etc. Must be good for you because I feel great physically.

Take care,

Don

Everything that goes around, comes around. I kept re-reading Don's letter. It's as though we're back to square one. As though he had just received his sentence. Fact is, it's 15 years and 2½ months since sentencing.

Bulletin: Greta Janusz died on January 19, 2011!

While all of this transpired, two Sundays ago I was driving south on the Sterling Highway with my fishing buddy, Andrew Gallagher. Our destination was the Kenai River. It felt like a Miami heatwave here in Alaska as temperatures flared to 42 degrees. We were planning to fish the daylight hours and catch a bounty of beautiful rainbow trout and Dollie Vardens.

Moving along on the southside of Cooper Landing, about five miles beyond the Russian River Ferry exit, I came upon a sharp, right-to-left curve, covered and camouflaged in black ice. I was well below the speed limit, but still lost control of my Subaru Outback. Hitting the brake would only make matters worse. Nothing I could do. We skidded across the highway, fortunate nothing was coming in the opposite direction. Way beyond fortunate, because the local newspaper *(Anchorage Daily News)* reported that earlier in the day the same thing happened to a woman driving the Sterling highway, losing control of her car, and colliding with another vehicle hauling a trailer headed in the opposite direction. The lady lost her life.

The most helpless feeling. So horrified I actually felt a split-second calmness. I recall saying to myself, "This is it." We proceeded down a snowy embankment on the other side of the road, the northbound side. Andrew said he saw a tree go by on our left. I didn't. Then, the car began to flip. Andrew thinks it happened three times. I cannot vouch for that. It all happened so fast.

I was aware but disorientated, the worst of sensations, being so out of control, hearing smashing and banging sounds, shattering windows, feeling glass shards. And then we came to a hard, abrupt stop, like slamming into a brick wall. I saw black for maybe two seconds. Then silence. The car came to rest lying on the passenger's side.

I heard Andrew moving about. He undid his seat belt and somehow fell on me, which to this day makes no sense. I'm thinking I should have fallen on him. He's yelling at me, "Are you alright? Are you alright?"

"I don't know. I don't know." I started feeling my face, neck, torso, looking down. All body parts seemed to be intact. No blood. Meanwhile, I'm yelling at Andrew, "Are you alright?"

"Yes. I think so." He rolled over me and opened my door, pushing hard because the car was lying on his side. "We gotta get outta here quick in case of leaking gas." He managed to work his way outside the car. I could see him on his feet. He appeared to be in good shape. Nervous, but OK. He held my door open. "C'mon David."

I tried to move out, but felt stiff. With difficulty, somehow Andrew freed me from the interior. We backed off and looked at each other, slowly realizing we would escape this horror show in one piece.

Several passing drivers stopped, offering assistance, which was very thoughtful, yet created a whole new threat from motorists winging and skidding around the deadly curve as we stood on the side of the road rounding up personal belongings, putting all in trash bags, and directing traffic. We set roadflares at the start and end of the curve. In time we were driven back to Anchorage. I am still shaky and spooked. Andrew is doing fine. The thought that I may have caused him injury bothers me to no end. We were having so much fun. We planned on taking the next left onto Skilak Lake Road. After traveling 110 miles we missed our destination by five miles. In just a matter of seconds, it could have been all over. We estimated from the beginning of our skid to the end, it took seven seconds. Thank God for seatbelts and the Subaru Outback, which is designed with top-notch safety reinforcements. Having collision insurance coverage also eased the pain.

Now, every morning upon waking I pinch myself. I give a hard pinch with my right thumb and index finger to a spot on the inside of my forearm. You know the spot. Mine has some developing redness from all the pinching. I am still here. So's Maureen, the dog and beautiful Alaska, my kids, my grandson... I'm a double-jeopardy victim, if you will, because I now have nightmares about the accident *and* Donald's tragedy. If you recall, going back to April of 2005, it was a nightmare about Don that generated my proactive role in trying to set him free.

January 20, 2011

Yesterday I replaced my 2006 Subaru Outback with the same model, only it's a deep-blue 2010. Beautiful car, better gas mileage, and just as sturdy. I'm very happy, very thankful. I completed all of the paperwork with Dave Smith, the Finance Director for Continental Subaru here in Anchorage. He's also a church preacher. We quickly discovered that we have a lot in common. Two Daves, Smith and Brown, the two most common surnames in America. We're both into sports, poker, reading and writing. He wanted to know all about Donald Graham. So, I gave him a thorough synopsis.

David Smith's first reply was, "Holy moley. What a story."

"What do you think?"

"I can tell this is an emotional experience for you, so much more subjective than objective. From the very beginning you took on a very defensive role for your friend, as though you were trying to convince me of his innocence. That's the key word, friend. How could you not? However, as I listened to the story unfold, I kept saying to myself, at every turn, at every move, Mr. Graham made choices. And each choice led to a sequence of bad events. That's my first reaction."

"Interesting."

"It got me to thinking, why the heck didn't he mind his own business? Ya know Dave, you hesitated when you said, 'At no time did Graham want to be behind the bad guy.' A choice. I understand had he gotten in front, he may have been rear-ended and driven off the road. However, what if he did get in front. He could have driven straight to the nearest police station. The bad guys may have had enough and driven off. We'll never know due to choice."

"This is true."

"Speaking of choices, who the heck carries a crossbow in their trunk over there in New England? Whole different ballgame up here in Alaska, ya know what I mean?"

David Smith paused. "Did you know that in most cases when someone takes another's life, the first thing they do is vomit? I read that somewhere. To kill takes both a mental and physical toll. It's the worst thing a person can possibly do. I've thought very deeply about murder, to the point that I believe if I caught a man raping my wife, I would not kill him. I certainly would want him to pay a price. But not murder. Let the judiciary system handle it. That's what they're for."

"I suspect if Don Graham were here, he'd be objecting and criticizing the Massachusetts system for railroading him."

"Probably would. You asked my opinion."

"Yes I did."

"And this happened, what, fifteen years ago?" Dave asked.

"February 20, 1994. You're close."

"That's a long time ago. Ya know, most stories change over time. I'm sure your friend goes over the details almost on a daily basis. Like a mark of Cain. I wonder if there are things he forgot. Things he may have slightly altered. That could be for self-preservation, for heavens sake. I don't know, just think-ing out loud."

"I understand. It's had me tearing my hair out for sixteen years now."

"Well, I'll tell you this. Based on what you've told me, I've come to the conclusion that first-degree murder was the correct sentence. It might not be what you want to hear; but, I'm a believer that we must strike hard at people who take lives."

"I'm surprised at your reaction, Dave," I replied. "Especially when you told me you're a Republican conservative. I figured you'd probably want to give Don a gold medal."

"I'm a retired preacher at the moment and a Republican fiscal conservative. Big on life. The likes of Donald Graham must pay a severe price."

"And you think first-degree, life without parole is justified?"

"Not the life without parole part. I think most everyone can be rehabili-tated. I think life with parole would have been the right sentence."

"I appreciate your opinion Dave. Unfortunately in the Commonwealth of Massachusetts first degree automatically includes life without."

"That's unfortunate."

"Sure is for Donald."

As I was leaving, Dave Smith called me back. "One more thing. I don't want you to get me wrong. I understand the tragedy and I have empathy for your friend. Yes, fate has dealt him a losing hand. But his life without parole has purpose, you know. He can make many worthy contributions to others in his time of incarceration."

Shakespeare wrote, "There is a tide in the affairs of men
Which taken at the flood, leads on to fortune."

We, the graduates, now find ourselves on the crest of that tide. We have the opportunities to let it bear us on the top of its crest to the fortune that can be ours, if we only have the ambition to seek it.

Success however, cannot be completely won unless we are also successful in finding a happy relationship with our fellow men. Money cannot buy true friends; so, for a person to be a complete success, he must also be a man of faith. His employer must have faith in his honesty and integrity. His friends must have faith in his friendship. His business associates must have faith in him to have faith in the product or company that he represents. He must have faith in himself and his own ideals. And, above all, faith in God.

Excerpts from Donald Graham's Class of 1957
Valedictorian speech, Peticodiac Regional High School.

Since my car accident, I've had thoughts that perhaps, just maybe, there was some form of divine intervention saving me from severe injury or even death. I know I came brutally close to buying the farm. Downright eerie and spooky to think that at one moment we're having a great time and in an instant everything turns horrific, as though the Devil himself appeared and stabbed us with his lethal pitchfork. A similar, yet more lethal, irony is what happened to Donald. Because of his road rage confrontation with Michael Blodgett, his life was completely rearranged, and he lives a daily nightmare. Perhaps it will take some form of divine intervention to set him free.

Not
The End

Postscript (November 2012)

I would be remiss if I did not share with you some recent activities. On October 12, 2012 Donald's new attorney, Patricia Quintilian, submitted a Motion for a New Trial to the Massachusetts Superior Court, Docket #BR34027. The Motion addresses the fact that the first day of trial was held in closed quarters, thus denying Donald his Constitutional rights to a public trial. It is a thorough 24-page document.

Don wrote to me on October 11, 2012 (excerpts):

> The court will assign the case to a judge. The judge will order the District Attorney's office to answer within a certain time frame. The DA's lawyers usually ask for several extensions of time to fix their answer and the court generally allows them the time. Once the appellate lawyer files his answer, my counsel has the right to shoot that answer down, maybe she'll ask for time also. Then the court can make a ruling on my Motion. The Supreme Judicial Court has never set any time frame in which the trial court must answer Rule 30 Motions. There are Motions that gather dust at the bottom of judges' inboxes. That's life.

> I have learned, and learned well, that any interloping Rhode Island Baptist deacon that interferes with a Massachusetts predator in the predator's pursuit of a female motorist, and who, in the protecting of himself and his spouse of 32 years, uses a crossbow to drive off his attackers, will soon find himself up to his righteous ass in the alligators of a Massachusetts witchhunt.

> In Massachusetts district attorneys are elected; they are politicians. When you mix politics and justice, you always get politics; justice becomes "JUST-US."

Often times, the solemn and definitive words of Donald's former attorney, Tom Dickinson, echo through my mind like the thump of a hallow gavel, "Manslaughter One, most likely Two." He nodded with surety. He gave me that reply on the day I asked him, in his opinion, did Don get what he deserved? Tom is now a probate and municipal court judge. I only wish he presided over Don's case. And Patricia Quintilian agrees. Recently she told me the Commonwealth pays $48,000 a year to keep her client behind bars.

From the beginning there have been two missions for *Deacon's Crossbow:* to get published, and raise enough public awareness to influence the Massachusetts judicial system to reduce or overturn Donald's sentence. Earlier this year I contacted a pen pal of Don's, Doreen Bradley from Woonsocket, who has taken a keen interest in his case. After several conversations and advice from colleagues, we are putting together a group with the objective of preparing a petition to present to Massachusetts Governor Deval Patrick asking for a commutation (a copy of *Deacon's Crossbow* has been forwarded to the governor). If all goes well, I look forward to flying back to New England and hand delivering the petition in person. If you would like to provide any suggestions or advice, please do so. Thank you.

Acknowledgements

Deacon's Crossbow has been a hard story to write. Time sensitive, sad and truly painful. Donald's experience has played upon my emotions, and in ways, has changed me forever. For example, I've never been especially sympathetic for the incarcerated. I'd been a believer that our justice system, by and large, works, and people sentenced to serve time deserve what they get. I'm not naive, I know there are exceptions. I just wanted to believe in our great country and the institutions we've so diligently created, like our justice system.

However, as a result of extensive research since the onset of this project, I've come to doubt the system and my altruistic attitude has changed. Our judicial system can do better by simply sticking to the guidelines and deferring from self-gain. The purpose of this book is not to instill hate or to "get someone." Yet *Deacon's* is a story of mistakes. I cannot stop repeating that Donald Graham's verdict was a mistake and every day I hope and pray it will be overturned.

Therefore, I want to first acknowledge compassion, and second, to recognize that we have the ability to change, to make laws more sensible and to ascertain that the right people are serving in the right place.

I also wish to acknowledge that conversations throughout are not always verbatim. But rest assured, the content and intent of each is spot on.

I want to thank all the key people I write about in the book from Donald, Rev. Roger Frances, Ed and Agnes Smith, private investigator Vic Pichette, the lawyers, Maureen and especially Vic Blank, as well as John Skowron, who wrote *Justice Denied ... The Crossbow Murder Case,* a thorough report about the incident. I covered every issue presented in that report.

Deacon's does not get past first base without critiques from my Anchorage writers group, Bill Coffey, and members of the Alaska Writers Guild. I must compliment Johanna Bohoy, a marvelous artist and graphic designer, for the work she did in preparing my book cover.

Lastly, I want to express my gratitude to Bob Golden, a longtime friend from Woonsocket, who is my business manager, critic, and the best proofreader I know.

From the Author

In 2005, I decided to do something about my friend, Donald S. Graham. *Deacon's Crossbow* is the end result. I spent six years gathering facts, interviewing, questioning and attempting to put my soul on printed paper.

Deacon's Crossbow represents my first published project of nonfiction.

All my previous published work was done as a freelancer for *The Woonsocket Call* (RI), as a columnist for the *Castro Valley Forum* (CA), and a columnist for the magazine, *Edibles East Bay* (CA). In 2005, I returned to college to immerse myself in selective creative writing courses at Cuesta College in Los Osos, CA. Loved every minute of it. In 2011, I served as president of the Alaska Writers Guild and continue to be their Program Director.

My portfolio also includes the forthcoming 375-page book of fiction, *Return of the Free Faller,* and a series which includes more than 75 short stories. I have also written a screenplay titled *Kinga.*

Originally from the "booming metropolis" of Woonsocket, RI, where I spent over 25 years as a businessman, I now live in Anchorage, AK.

David G. Brown

Made in the USA
Charleston, SC
29 April 2014